Do You Feel Like You Wasted All That Training?

Michael J. McLaughlin, MD

Do You Feel Like You Wasted All That Training?

Copyright ©2007 by Michael J. McLaughlin, MD.

This book is dedicated to physicians considering a career transition; to relatives, friends, and colleagues who have supported my career and my writing and who provided input on this book; to Bill for all of his guidance through the transition process and beyond; to my business partner Carolyn for making our work enjoyable; and to Kristin, Megan, Amelia, and Carolyn for helping me keep everything in perspective.

AUTOBIOGRAPHICAL NOTE

In March of 2001 I did what was considered by many of my peers to be the unthinkable; I left my plastic surgery practice of four years at the age of 36 to begin working in medical communications. If you are a physician reading this and are not familiar with the field of medical communications, there is no reason to worry; you are not alone. Until one year before my career transition, I had never heard of my current industry.

By 1999 I was in a highly specialized surgical field, wanted to do something different with my life, and had no idea where to start. I then spent most of my spare time during the last two years of my surgical practice struggling to identify and explore alternative career paths. At first I did not know about the large number of industries that required physician expertise or where to find out about them. Most importantly, I did not know anyone in these industries. It was only through the mentoring of a relative who had made his own successful clinical-to-non-clinical career transition that I formulated a plan of attack. Eventually I learned about the education, advertising, and publication planning opportunities available within the medical communications industry.

Now, as co-owner of Peloton Advantage, a medical communications company, I frequently interact with physicians in non-clinical jobs, as well as countless clinicians who are interested in career transition. Although I once considered myself an anomaly, I now have a better sense of the growing number of physicians in non-clinical jobs and the even larger number of opportunities available. Unfortunately, an organized approach to bring these groups of physicians together has been lacking.

Several widely varying industries have increasing demands for medical expertise in both full-time and consulting capacities. Companies in the pharmaceutical, communications, insurance, legal, public health, investment, publishing, and creative industries have constant need for such expertise. There are numerous opportunities in research, hospital administration, public health, and non-profit organizations as well. Numerous demands for medical expertise exist outside of clinical practice; the challenge is finding them.

The number of physicians working and consulting in non-clinical jobs continues to rise. Students and residents are increasingly evaluating such opportunities, and many older physicians are reducing the percentage of their time in the clinic, or retiring from practice earlier to pursue these options. Even more profound, however, is the rapidly rising number of physicians exploring such alternatives midstream in their careers.

The supply of physician expertise and the demand for this resource are equally impressive but at times appear to be divided by an impassable chasm. Most physicians do not know what their non-clinical options are, let alone where and how to begin searching. Even physicians who have entered a non-clinical industry have minimal opportunity to learn about other types of non-clinical jobs. There is a large unmet need for cross-pollination of ideas and opportunities within the non-clinical arena.

In 2004 I founded Physician Renaissance Network, a comprehensive resource for doctors with non-clinical jobs and interests, or a desire to explore such options. Physician Renaissance Network focuses on education, career development, and networking opportunities. For now I write the majority of the content for the web site (www.prnresource.com) but also encourage participation and interaction by physician visitors. This involvement has been particularly rewarding to me. I can relate to the obstacles faced by physicians visiting the site and hope to facilitate the evolution of their careers.

While speaking with many practicing clinicians considering a career transition, I have been impressed by how similar their challenges and questions are. By writing this book of my answers to these commonly asked questions, I hope to help physicians who are in the situation where I once found myself. I hope that the readers will find some additional direction and practical advice in the pages that follow. I welcome reader feedback and ideas and encourage you to contact me through the Physician Renaissance Network web site.

THE JOURNEY

QUESTION

I don't even know where to start. Did you follow a process?

ANSWER

Yes, there was a process. I initially floundered through my search, getting ahead of myself, only to find that I was moving inefficiently and often in the wrong direction. This improved dramatically once adhering to a five phase process: introspection, exploration, preparation, acquisition, and transition.

Introspection set the stage for the subsequent phases. I had to do some soul searching to decide why I was considering a career transition and what I was hoping to find. Force-ranking the characteristics of my ideal job was necessary before searching for one that matched my priorities.

Exploration was the most time consuming phase, involving extensive research of various types in order to establish the realm of non-clinical possibilities available to physicians. Using the lessons learned from my introspection, I continuously assessed these potential types of positions, using my personalized list of ideal job characteristics. I gradually honed in on a specific industry and then a specific type of position that would suit my ability and interests.

Preparation involved taking a hard look at the requirements for the positions I was considering and assessing my expertise. There were gaps, such as the limited depth of my writing experience, that I had to fill in order to increase my marketability.

It was not until these phases were complete that I was fully prepared to acquire a new position. *Acquisition* was where I wanted to start before getting better advice, and where many physicians considering a career transition often mistakenly start. Looking right away at job opportunities before considering what you really want and what the options are may actually lead to a new job, but it is far less likely to lead to the best job.

Transition involves a combination of emotional and practical elements that are equally important to consider in advance. This phase starts toward the end of the clinical practice period and extends for a variable amount of time until you are established at the new position. First, you should establish a plan for the continued care of your patients. As far as your own career path, it is important to avoid burning any bridges during this time. While returning to clinical practice may be undesirable, this option provides a safety net as you make the transition.

Networking is crucial throughout the process and improves the efficiency of navigating through these five phases.

Figure 1. Career Transition Process

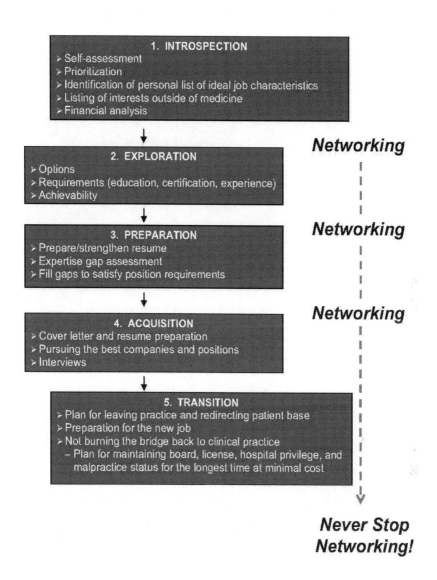

1. INTROSPECTION
- Self-assessment
- Prioritization
- Identification of personal list of ideal job characteristics
- Listing of interests outside of medicine
- Financial analysis

↓

Networking

2. EXPLORATION
- Options
- Requirements (education, certification, experience)
- Achievability

↓

Networking

3. PREPARATION
- Prepare/strengthen resume
- Expertise gap assessment
- Fill gaps to satisfy position requirements

↓

Networking

4. ACQUISITION
- Cover letter and resume preparation
- Pursuing the best companies and positions
- Interviews

↓

5. TRANSITION
- Plan for leaving practice and redirecting patient base
- Preparation for the new job
- Not burning the bridge back to clinical practice
  - Plan for maintaining board, license, hospital privilege, and malpractice status for the longest time at minimal cost

Never Stop Networking!

QUESTION
How long did you know that you wanted to leave clinical practice?

ANSWER

Deciding to leave clinical practice was a gradual process occurring over several years, rather than an overnight realization that I should make a change. I suppose that I had some thoughts about an alternative career path as early as my internship. That timing probably does not shock a lot of physicians: I am sure that the internship year is a defining period for many people.

I knew from an early age that I wanted to go into medicine. When I was a junior in high school I decided to become a cardiac surgeon. My drive to become a surgeon would affect nearly every decision I made during the years of school and training that followed.

There were several times when my eagerness to become a physician threatened to propel me forward too fast. I considered combined medical programs straight out of high school; instead, I chose to go to Harvard for my undergraduate degree. Even there, I considered an accelerated program that would have allowed me to graduate in three years and get into medical school earlier, but wisely changed my mind. The emphasis of my curriculum involved premedical studies. I majored in biology. I did genetics research that led to a thesis. I did everything necessary to improve my medical school application.

I went to medical school at Columbia University's College of Physicians and Surgeons in New York City. There I did research in cardiac surgery and transplantation. I also spent a fair amount of my spare time working with the cardiac transplantation team, flying in the middle of the night to various places to assist with organ harvests. When applying for residency, I again considered combined programs that would have included nine or ten years in general and cardiothoracic surgery, but instead I chose to stay at Columbia for the five-year general surgery program.

Hospital rotations and internship provided a closer look at the day-to-day life of surgeons in different specialties. Getting married between medical school and internship also altered my perspective on the future. In high school I thought in terms of one person; now I was viewing my career from the perspective of a husband and future father. While I had a great deal of respect for the cardiothoracic surgeons with whom I worked, I was able to see the time commitment that their careers required and the impact on their family lives.

As all of these factors converged during internship, I realized that I no longer wanted to be a cardiothoracic surgeon. This was a defining moment in my career. Cardiac surgery had consumed my plans for more than a decade. If not that, then what? There were brief moments when I considered the concept of non-clinical options, but everything I could imagine remained within the realm of surgery. I was so busy and exhausted that I rarely had enough time to truly think through what my overall options were. It never occurred to me that my future might lie outside of   surgery.

During the next few years, two of my best friends left our residency program for non-clinical jobs. The first left after her internship to write consumer healthcare books. The other left after his second year of residency and entered the pharmaceutical industry. After watching them leave and talking to them about how happy they were with their decision, I occasionally wondered if such an alternative might be an option for me. At that time, however, I could still not envision such a path for my career. Also, as a resident, I was mainly doing the more interesting and rewarding aspects of a surgeon's job. I spent a great deal of my time operating. Managed care headaches, piles of paperwork, and the threat of lawsuits had not yet found me.

During my third year of general surgery residency, I decided to become a hand surgeon. Three training paths can lead to a hand surgery fellowship, one of which is plastic surgery. Columbia had a strong plastic surgery program that accepted applicants after only three years of general surgery, rather than the standard five. I was fortunate enough to get one of the two positions for that two-year program.

Every year generated more doubt about my future career path. I kept optimistically reassuring myself, however, that each "next year" of residency training would be more rewarding and bring me closer to the culmination of my hard work – a career in surgery. This continued through all five years of training at Columbia and then at the subsequent year at the University of Utah during my hand surgery and microsurgery fellowship.

I remember signing the employer agreement to join the multi-specialty group in Bethlehem,

PA, and questioning whether practicing surgery was the correct direction for me. I still had no idea what else I could do. I had spent the last 14 years learning and training pursuing this particular career path and never imagined how such skills could transfer to a different type of job. I was at a point where I would soon find out what it was really like to be a fully trained surgeon, and was willing to give that a try.

After two years in practice, I passed my plastic surgery and hand surgery boards on schedule and was admitted to the most prestigious associations in my field. Ironically, the completion of that process, the culmination of all of my studies and training, coincided with my decision to leave clinical practice.

I was 33 years old and married with two daughters. I was finally certain that I wanted to leave clinical practice. What were my options? What could I do? What did I want to do?

QUESTION

Did you know many physicians who made a similar career transition?

ANSWER

No, especially early in my career.

I have to recount a story from when I was twenty one years old, just to demonstrate how much my thoughts on this subject have changed over time. I worked as a lifeguard at our community pool in the summer between college and medical school. I was speaking to a gentleman in his forties one day and mentioned that I was headed to medical school. He told me that he used to be a cardiologist but did not enjoy it and left his practice. The concept of not wanting to be a practicing physician anymore was mind-boggling to me, and I was disappointed that he would do such a thing. I assumed that there was something wrong with him. I do not know why I made that assumption, but I did. Maybe I had a naïve and idealized view of clinical practice at that time. Fifteen years later I left my own practice.

My interest in writing shone a spotlight on some physician authors. I went to the same medical school where Robin Cook had gone. I read a lot of Robin Cook's books and was always intrigued by the concept that a physician could become that successful as a writer. I have also been a big fan of Michael Crichton, whose creative talents have extended from books to television and movies.

I did a fourth-year medical school emergency room rotation at Vanderbilt University during the peak of my cardiothoracic transplant surgery aspirations. I was very interested in the surgery program there and scheduled time to speak with Dr. William Frist, a cardiothoracic transplant surgeon. Despite his hectic schedule, Dr. Frist was generous with his time as we discussed several topics, including my future goals and his surgical experience. I was quite impressed with Dr. Frist, a man who appeared to have so much of what I sought for my future, not to mention an easy-going elegance and charisma.

Dr. Frist gave me a copy of his book, *Transplant: A Heart Surgeon's Account of the Life-And-Death Dramas of the New Medicine*. I read the book, an autobiography focused on his life as a cardiothoracic surgeon, while imagining myself in that role. One chapter includes a detailed description of Dr. Frist returning from the hospital in the middle of the night and noticing how much his young child had grown since he was last home. At the time, I thought his account was exaggerated, but I later had flashbacks to this chapter during my internship when returning home to my wife and infant daughter following weekend-long calls in the hospital.

It was eye-opening to watch Dr. Frist on the news a few years later, leaving cardiothoracic surgery for the United States Senate. By that time I had already discarded my plans to become a cardiothoracic surgeon, and was even considering non-clinical options. For me, Dr. Frist exemplified the feasibility of transitioning from one successful career path to another.

During my residency training, I got to know Dr. Neil Shulman, a cardiologist from Emory University who has been successful in numerous endeavors outside of clinical medicine. Neil's academic success includes many research projects and publications and extensive experience in preventive medicine and patient education, particularly in the area of hypertension and kidney and heart disease.

Neil is a well known speaker and entertainer. He has published seventeen books including *Your Body's Red Light Warning Signals: Medical Tips That May Save Your Life*, and *Your Body, Your Health: How to Ask Questions, Find Answers, and Work with Your Doctor*. He has written, produced and acted in videos and movies. The movie *Doc Hollywood* was based on his novel *What? Dead Again?* He also has been instrumental in creating charitable organizations.

Neil was an inspiration to me. Within a few seconds of meeting him, I marveled at his ingenuity and seemingly endless energy. He can breathe life into ideas that others would not even recognize as being possible. When I spoke to him about some of my aspirations, even the ones that I considered to be a bit far-fetched, he took them seriously and made me even more confident that I could achieve those goals.

Earlier I mentioned two colleagues who left our surgery residency for non-clinical jobs. Soon I will discuss the impact that a non-clinical physician relative had on my career transition.

QUESTION

Did you have a career coach?

ANSWER

I know other physicians who have sought the service of a general career coach, but I did not. Luckily, a relative served as a mentor and remained dedicated to helping me through the entire career transition process. Having a physician who could serve as a role model and fully understand what was driving me was extremely beneficial. I have now advised numerous physicians through the career transition process.

QUESTION
How did your mentor help you?

ANSWER

Having a career transition mentor was the most important factor that enabled me to complete the process.

My brother-in-law's father is a physician who left his residency training to start an emergency room physician staffing company. He enjoyed personal and financial success through the growth and sale of the company. Since that time he has successfully started and managed other companies, and has been involved in several philanthropic activities.

He was well aware of my frustration with clinical practice from several years of discussing the topic, and was very eager to help when I decided to explore alternative options. He recommended that we meet every other week at a point approximately halfway between our homes in Bethlehem and Philadelphia. For the next two years, we met at a restaurant to discuss my desired career transition.

At first I recounted a litany of reasons why I wanted to leave my current job, without a goal in sight. This was a particularly emotional time for me, because I felt trapped in a dead end – as though all of my hard work, studying and training, was wasted. Worst of all, I did not see a way out. During the first several meetings, my mentor convinced me of three beliefs necessary to begin the transition process: 1) that there were non-clinical jobs requiring my skills, 2) that I could fill in the remaining gaps in my skills and transfer them to such a job, and

3) that I could overcome the likely financial challenge associated with such a transition.

The fourth belief had to come from within – I had to believe in myself. I think if that was not the case, I would have given up many times along the way.

We discussed the realities that I had to accept. This transition was not going to be easy or fast. I would have to be as dedicated to this process as I was to becoming a physician many years earlier. I also had to be willing to begin at the bottom of the totem pole again. That was a reality that would affect me psychologically and financially.

My mentor provided a structure to the career transition process, which consisted of five phases: introspection, exploration, preparation, and acquisition, and transition. We worked through this sequence methodically, with homework assignments that I completed between meetings. Over time we honed in on a target industry and position while walking through the steps necessary to get there. Many dinners later, I made an extremely rewarding career transition. I realize how fortunate I was to have guidance through that process and understand that most people do not have access to such an advisor.

Hopefully this book will help provide a reasonable surrogate for a mentor and an organized approach to non-clinical career path exploration. In my opinion, however, there is no true substitute for the guidance gained from two-way discussion with a mentor.

QUESTION

How long did it take to make the career transition?

ANSWER

Once I decided that I definitely wanted to make a career transition, it took about two years to get a non-clinical job.

QUESTION

Why did it take so long to make the transition?

ANSWER

At first glance, the two years probably seems like a long time. Living through it certainly felt endless at the time.

I attribute the amount of time to several factors. First of all, prior to the point of deciding that I wanted to pursue a new job, I was so busy trying to make my clinical practice successful that I had limited time to spare. Deciding to explore alternative options threw open a door that I had never even noticed before. I had to start from scratch. Even after deciding to leave clinical practice, I was still fairly busy with my "day job." This practical challenge became especially frustrating. Unlike the way this would be depicted in a novel or movie, I was not in a financial position to walk away from my practice and "find myself." Through after-hours search efforts, I gathered information from multiple parallel processes, including regular meetings with my mentor, networking, and online research.

During these two years of exploring alternative options, I followed a systematic process of exploring potential job types, identifying my areas of interest, and pursuing a position. This process was more involved and time consuming than I would have imagined. Without a methodical approach to this task, however, it is very likely that my career transition would not have happened, or perhaps even worse – that I might have entered a similarly non-satisfying position in a different industry.

Networking required a great deal of effort to overcome the initial inertia and place

27

the gears in motion. In the beginning I was only contacting one or two people every couple of weeks. As a result, it took several months before I was speaking to people who could directly influence my career path. Once I established a network of people in medical communications, my area of interest, I had to wait for new positions to become available.

My online research was particularly inefficient. Much of the problem was caused by searching for open positions before I had spent adequate time fully understanding which types of jobs were best for me. I did not realize until afterwards that I applied for several positions that did not require medical expertise and therefore did not meet my salary threshold. There are a handful of well-defined job titles that are appropriate for physicians within the pharmaceutical and medical communications industries. Unless you know what these are, or have someone who can help direct you toward them, trying to match your skill set to these jobs is equivalent to finding a needle in a haystack.

I now look back on the amount of time that it took me to hone in on hand surgery – the last two years of high school, four years of college, four years of medical school, and the first three years of my surgical training – and understand that the two years I spent evaluating and entering this new industry were actually relatively efficient and quite successful.

Five years after making the transition, I was a satisfied business owner with a positive outlook on my future. Becoming established in my new career took far less time than the effort involved to begin practicing medicine.

Figure 2. Author's Career Timeline

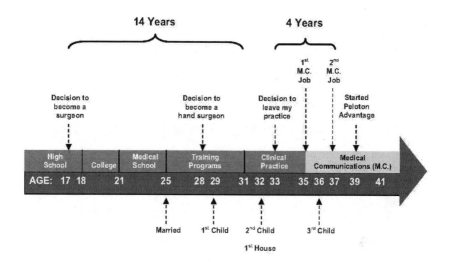

QUESTION

How long did you know you wanted to go into medical communications?

ANSWER

When I was in clinical practice and was just starting to consider alternative options, I did not know that the field of medical communications existed. As with many physicians, my interactions with the pharmaceutical industry mainly involved having sales representatives come to my office, or attending an occasional dinner meeting. I never gave much thought to how those meetings and materials were developed. I assumed at that time that the pharmaceutical companies did all this work themselves. Much of this work is actually out-sourced.

It was only through my exploration of alternative career paths that I learned about all of the different companies that provide products and services to the pharmaceutical companies (eg, contract research, medical communications, and market research). Medical communications made the most sense to me because I was looking to combine my medical expertise and writing skills.

I began to hone in on medical communications a few months after deciding to explore non-clinical options. I started my first job in that industry about 18 months later.

INTROSPECTION

QUESTION

How did you decide what you wanted to do?

ANSWER

The first step in deciding on a different career path is to prioritize the goals for the next job. This sounded simple at first, and I thought I knew exactly what was important to me, but I agreed with my mentor to make this a mandatory assignment. Once I actually took the time to sit down with a pencil and paper and write out the list, I surprised myself. It was also important to get my wife involved in this step to review my list. It was necessary to discuss these priorities together as early in the search process as possible.

Before diving into what I wanted in a future job, I took a look at my current job as a practicing surgeon. I listed the positive aspects of my job, and then the negative aspects. My initial "positive" list included the following items:

- Intellectually challenging
- Technically challenging
- Generally highly respected career
- Good current salary
- High earning potential
- Doing good for people

My initial "negative" list included:

- Long hours
- Insurance company restrictions
- Patient demands
- Pressure of the consequences of a bad result
- Concern about   malpractice threat

- Malpractice and other overhead costs
- Yielding a high percentage of my "profit" to the practice

When I thought more about these and got more specific, it helped further assess my job. For example, "long hours" really broke out into several items that provided much more insight into why I wanted to leave clinical practice:

- Unpredictability of work hours
- Getting called back into the office during dinner
- Being on call
- Lack of sleep
- Lack of sufficient coverage to leave town
- Interruptions of time with my family
- The threat of interruptions while enjoying time with my family

These started to add up to lack of control over my work time, which impacted on the quality of my "free time."

I did my best to complete these lists and then revisited them as I proceeded with my exploration of alternative career paths. In looking back now, I realize that I completely missed one of the best aspects of clinical practice – job security. I never had to worry about the possibility of being laid off. The thought probably does not even enter the minds of most physicians; in most cases it probably feels like their job is secure, 24 hours a day, 7 days a week, including holidays. In non-clinical industries, however, I have seen physicians fired and laid off. The impact of such events cannot be overstated.

Next, without a specific job in mind, I used my current "positives" and "negatives" to create a new list of the attributes that I desired in my next job. It was not very difficult to come up with the list of attributes. The difficult part was taking this list and translating the specifics into what they really meant. For example, "doing good for people" and "generally highly respected career" fell under a bigger heading of job "fulfillment" – a sense of accomplishment. Most of the items on my "negatives" list suggested inadequate "control" over my life, in many cases the balance of career and family. The ideal job had to take these items into account, rather than specifically reducing my battles with insurance companies or eliminating the cost of malpractice.

Then came the big challenge: prioritization. I had to force-rank and narrow the list. I had to be honest with myself. It might be nice to tell people that the reason I went into medicine was to help people (which is the truth), but I did not even want to think about reducing my salary – by 10%, by 25%, especially by 50%. Which items on the list did I have to have? What could I do without, if I had to choose?

I think that making and revisiting these lists are helpful during the search process. In the end, walking through this exercise may help assure you that practicing medicine, while not perfect, achieves more of your top objectives than any alternative that you are considering. Then you can refocus on your clinical practice with extra peace of mind. There is certainly benefit in such confirmation, not to mention the time saved wandering down a dead-end job search.

With my lists in hand, I started looking into alternative career path options that matched my priorities.

Figure 3. Comparing Clinical Practice to Your Optimal Job

My List

Optimal Job Characteristics	Clinical Practice Scores
Intellectual Challenge	4/5
Team Environment	2/5
Sense of Accomplishment	4/5
Financial Reward	3/5
Manageable Workload	2/5
Schedule Control	1/5
TOTAL	16/30

Your List

Optimal Job Characteristics	Clinical Practice Scores
?	/5
?	/5
?	/5
?	/5
?	/5
?	/5
TOTAL	/30

It is important for others to understand that honing in on my first non-clinical position involved a fair amount of trial and error. As methodical as I like to think I am, I have to admit that I did not systematically identify each subsequent step in the search process and propel myself toward it like a laser beam. My feeling, however, is that if you move too quickly and easily toward a new job, there is probably a good chance that you have overlooked something. Mistakes are okay, as long as you recognize them, back away, and readjust your direction.

A major part of my trial and error was due to a limited understanding of what the job specifications and background requirements were for some positions. For example, I began looking for medical editor positions. While my medical background would provide some degree of benefit in this position, much of my expertise was superfluous to the actual requirements of the job. I also far underestimated the amount of skill and expertise that goes into being an editor and my ability to transition into this job and do it well. As a result, my salary requirement was too high, my ability to perform well in that job was quite limited, and I do not think any employer would have taken me seriously for these positions. Not realizing this, I applied for a few editor positions and even took an editing test for one company. By the way, in case you were wondering, I bombed the test.

My first position outside of clinical practice was as an Associate Medical Director at a medical communications company in New Jersey. This position fulfilled the majority of the line items on my priority list. I would be using my medical background. The job was intellectually challenging. I enjoyed the people and the team environment in the company. The hours at this entry level position were fewer and more predictable than my surgery hours. Weekends and vacations would be beeper-free ("priceless," as they say in the television ads).

I am sure that all of this sounds wonderful, but no job is perfect.

The salary, while a 33% drop from my salary in practice, was what I had anticipated in an entry level position following a career transition. Also, the management team at the new company helped outline a salary increase schedule that would get me back above my break-even point within two years.

I had a 90 minute commute to get to work each day. This was obviously a major drawback, but a price that I was willing to pay in exchange for the other benefits of the job. Of course I had the option of relocating, which I decided not to do until becoming fully established in medical communications.

Perhaps most importantly, I was confident that I could fulfill the job requirements and perform well in this new industry. This helped to allay the uncertainty that is probably always present when someone makes a significant career transition.

QUESTION

How did you decide how much money you wanted to make?

ANSWER

I did not decide how much money I *wanted* to make, but rather how much money I *needed* to make. It was important to me to support my family's lifestyle without them feeling the impact of my new salary.

In many respects, the first few years in a new position would be on-the-job training. I accepted that I would be making less money during this time. Compared to the number of years that I had to spend in residency programs at very low pay before becoming an attending physician, I would be getting a bargain.

How much did I need to make? My wife and I went back through our previous year's credit card bills and checking account statements and calculated our expenses within several general categories. We then factored in increasing costs such as projected tuition for the kids. Other expenses such as automotive/gas would increase with the long commute. Only my medical school loan payments, which were mercifully drawing close to completion, would actually decrease. These budgets allowed us to project our anticipated expenses for the next two years. We then added in a $10,000 margin of error on top of this figure. Correcting for income taxes brought us to the base salary that I would require in order to cover our cost of living. This was what I considered to be my "break even point."

It did not take much exploration of non-clinical options before I realized that getting a starting salary that exceeded my break-even point would be a challenge. My wife and I discussed how much of our savings we would be willing to use to cover our expenses and decided on a lower salary that we could tolerate for a specified amount of time. This knowledge helped a great deal when negotiating my starting salary and performance review schedule with my new company.

Luckily my new boss was a reasonable person, and we had an honest discussion about my financial situation. I explained that I was willing to take a lower initial salary as a cost of entry into a new industry, but that unless I exceeded a specific threshold in salary within the first year, I would not be able to continue working with them. As a result, we were able to work through a starting salary with two tentative increases based on my performance during the course of the first year. I was able to get the timing of two accelerated performance reviews in writing and had a verbal agreement with my manager regarding the salary increases. Making an important agreement on a handshake is generally not recommended, but I had faith in my new boss. As a general rule, companies avoid making performance-dependent promises in writing, and this was the case with the company that was hiring me.

The business world almost taught me a harsh lesson when my new boss left the company one month after I was hired. One day he was in the office, and the next day he was gone. Several of his verbal agreements seemed lost in transition when I later discussed them with the remaining managers. Luckily, my boss made sure to pass along the salary commitment to the remainder of the senior management team. We were able to work through these details in a way that met my expectations.

Through a great deal of hard work and strong performance reviews, I was able to deliver on my promise to the company, and they in turn provided me with the two salary increases on schedule. As a result, within the first year in my new job, I was earning a salary at $10,000 less than my defined "break even point." With some more hard work, I would cross that threshold as well.

QUESTION

How did you decide on medical communications?

ANSWER

I have loved to write since I was a young child. I still have a collection of short stories that I wrote when I was about eight years old. Despite majoring in biology and focusing on pre-medical subjects in college, my two most memorable courses were poetry writing and fiction writing, which took place in small interactive workshop settings. Since that time, I have written numerous short pieces within several genres, some of which have made it to print. I now have several drafts of novel manuscripts in various stages, including a few that I have completed.

Writing was always an enjoyable part of my work as a physician. In medical school and during residency I enjoyed writing several clinical articles, as well as a few editorials that were published in medical journals. While in practice I wrote regularly for two web sites, www.personalmd.com and www.suite101.com.

When I started to explore the possibility of a different job, I had no idea that the area of medical communications existed. I learned about this industry through my networking and research process. As soon as I realized that there might be a way for me to combine my medical background and love for writing, I knew that this was the direction to focus my quest.

Many physicians considering a career transition want to continue utilizing their medical background. The desire to leverage the amount of medical

42

knowledge gained throughout the years is quite reasonable. Also, we went into medicine because of a passion for the subject, for both intellectual and emotional reasons. There is no need to leave behind this passion when turning toward a non-clinical option.

For me the possibility of combining two passions into a single career path was an exciting epiphany and continues to be rewarding.

EXPLORATION

QUESTION

Did you consider ways to improve your clinical practice situation, rather than making a career transition?

ANSWER

Yes, absolutely. Missing the opportunity to improve an existing job would have been an egregious oversight. I considered many less dramatic options before choosing to enter a new industry. In fact, I made some adjustments in my call and office schedule that improved my situation while searching for a new job.

Remaining in my existing practice and making changes necessary to improve my situation was the first option that I weighed. Maybe I could eliminate emergency room call, take Wednesdays off, stop accepting HMO or Workers Compensation patients, or even switch to a purely cosmetic surgery practice. These were just a few of the options that I considered. The problem was that none of those options would have gotten me close enough to the ideal job attributes that I listed in the introspection phase.

I also considered alternative clinical practice options. Joining another private practice did not seem to provide much benefit. I wondered if moving to a different location, such as Montana where some colleagues were practicing, might improve enough aspects of clinical practice that I would enjoy what I was doing. I kept asking myself that question, but decided that I was more likely to end up in the wrong job *and* the wrong location if I made such a change. I considered going into academic medicine but still favored private practice over that option.

Starting a solo practice was an option, of course. The non-competition clause in my contract would have forced me outside of a certain radius from my existing practice. It did not matter much, though. Starting a solo practice would not have addressed the issues that made me unhappy in the group practice setting, and start-up costs, including malpractice, would have put me further in debt.

From that point, I considered a myriad of other possibilities that physicians typically do. These included taking on occasional locum tenens work, working in an emergency room, and changing specialties, just to name a few.

I continued to weigh a few of these options as I explored non-clinical alternatives. When I learned about medical communications, however, I left all of these less satisfying possibilities behind. By that point, I already made the mental transition; now it was just a matter of time before the new job became a reality.

Figure 4. Assessing Alternative Paths

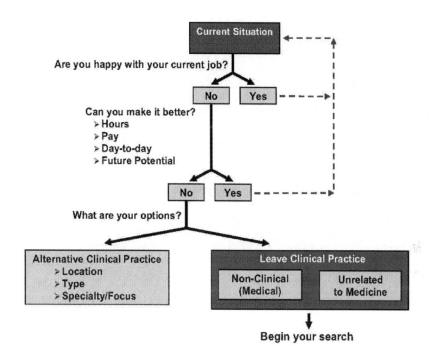

QUESTION

What are my options outside of clinical practice?

ANSWER

The non-clinical options for a physician are truly endless.

There are a few initial questions that you should ask yourself to narrow the focus. First you need to decide if you want to do something medical. While most physicians transitioning from clinical practice can find the best opportunity by leveraging their medical and scientific backgrounds, many select areas that are quite remote from medicine. Another important question is whether you want to be an employee or own your own business. Some physicians are averse to accepting an entry level position in a new industry after managing their own practice.

We should first discuss non-clinical jobs in which you can most directly leverage your medical experience. Hospital administration is one such option and may provide a stepwise career transition, rather than an abrupt change. We all have a general understanding of university faculty positions and various types of research opportunities, which are options commonly pursued by clinical physicians looking for a transition.

The pharmaceutical industry is a large area that consists not only of the pharmaceutical companies themselves, but also the peripheral industries to which pharmaceutical companies out-source work, such as contract research organizations (CROs), medical advertising, medical communications, and contract sales organizations (CSOs). Within pharmaceutical companies, some of the most common positions exist in medical affairs, regulatory affairs, medical marketing and communications, research and development, and clinical development.

The insurance industry hires physicians as Medical Directors to establish and evaluate treatment guidelines, as well as to review member claims. Physicians working part-time in clinical practice can perform Independent Medical Evaluations (IMEs) for insurance companies and/or legal firms.

Many physicians work in the legal industry and are generally hired by law firms on a case-by-case basis. In this role as an expert witness, physicians prepare reports after reviewing medical charts and provide testimony in courtroom cases. Some physicians choose to get a law degree and use their combined MD/JD to enter related areas of law, such as malpractice claims or intellectual property for medical equipment, devices or pharmaceuticals.

Stock brokerages and investment banks hire physicians as analysts for their expertise in assessing companies that provide services or make products for the healthcare industry. A few large venture capital and private equity companies hire physicians for similar purposes. In these positions, physicians combine their medical knowledge and investment market skills to review companies based on their individual products or portfolio, generating reports that include projected sales, stock value, and buy/sell recommendations.

There are also numerous opportunities in the public health arena. These range from working in a city's department of health, to positions at the state or federal level. There are also many positions at the National Institutes of Health (NIH) and the Centers for Disease Control and Prevention (CDC).

Physicians have become successful news reporters. In fact, the American Medical Association has hosted an annual Health Reporting Conference for physicians who also work as medical reporters, or are interested in this career.

Medical publishing holds a variety of opportunities. There are positions for physicians on the editorial staff and boards of journals. Numerous physicians also write textbooks and other health-related books. This is another area that may allow a gradual transition or a part-time position.

Some medical associations and other non-profit organizations have physicians on staff. In addition, there are countless volunteer opportunities for physicians looking to combine their medical background with philanthropic interests.

There are opportunities within the creative arts. Many physicians have written works of fiction and nonfiction, as well as scripts for the television and movie industry. The success of physicians such as Michael Crichton, Robin Cook, Neil Shulman, Michael Palmer and Tess Gerritsen highlight such avenues for creative writing. Numerous physicians involved in sculpture, painting, and other creative arts bring their unique medical perspective to their work. Famous members and past presidents of the American Physicians Art Association have included Drs. Alma Dea Morani, Meyer M. Melicow, and Rise Delmar Ochsner.

The non-medical opportunities for physicians leaving practice are endless. There are physician business owners in all walks of life, from restaurateurs to sculptors. Dr. William Frist left his cardiothoracic surgery practice to become a U.S. Senator, and Dr. Howard Brush Dean III is Chairman of the National Democratic Committee and a former U.S. presidential candidate. Dr. Thomas J. Fogarty, inventor of the Fogarty balloon embolectomy catheter, owns a vineyard in California. If it can be done, it can be done by a physician who has left clinical practice. The goal is to align such an option with your interests and skill set.

Figure 5. Non-Clinical Possibilities

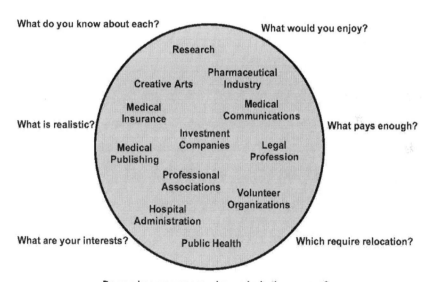

What do you know about each?

What would you enjoy?

What is realistic?

What pays enough?

Research

Pharmaceutical Industry

Creative Arts

Medical Insurance

Medical Communications

Investment Companies

Medical Publishing

Legal Profession

Professional Associations

Volunteer Organizations

Hospital Administration

What are your interests?

Public Health

Which require relocation?

Do you know someone who works in these areas?

QUESTION

What medical specialties are in highest demand?

ANSWER

A career transition can be made from any specialty, since physicians are in high demand in non-clinical jobs across numerous therapeutic categories. Different positions may require specialty expertise or a more general background. As a result, there are career path strategies that remain focused within a specialty and others that aim for a broad range of experience.

Certain areas such as cardiology, oncology, neurology, and psychiatry are the leaders in drug development and generate the highest pharmaceutical sales. This trend affects hiring patterns by pharmaceutical companies and the satellite industries that provide services to them. Extensive clinical trials being done in these areas leads to increased involvement of contract research organizations (CROs). Ever emerging treatment options in these areas result in increased need for educational programs and materials. Also, financial analysts generally focus a lot of effort in these areas, making expertise in such specialties an asset.

It is helpful to understand when certain specialty expertise is required for a particular position. If the job description states that the company is looking for a cardiologist and that is not your specialty, then it is highly unlikely that you would be considered for that position and it is most likely a waste of your time to apply.

It may be preferable for a physician to have their new job focus within their previous area of practice, especially in cases where such specialty expertise can justify a higher salary. A specialist may also be successful at a job that requires general medical knowledge, although perhaps at a salary negotiation disadvantage.

My specialty expertise in plastic surgery and hand surgery has not provided a noticeable benefit in medical communications. In fact, I felt as though these particular specialties reduced my initial options. Employers labeled me as a specialist, rather than how I saw myself – a well educated physician able to refresh my memory and get up to speed quickly on any medical subject.

Although I was able to make a career transition to a position where I was initially working on a plastic surgery account, I quickly realized the importance of expanding my medical communications experience. I took every opportunity to work on other types of products, soon generating a broad portfolio. This allowed me to strengthen my expertise across numerous therapeutic areas, rather than being labeled simply as a plastic surgeon.

QUESTION

What types of resources are available to explore non-clinical options?

ANSWER

Physicians are used to linear career paths, formalized educational programs, and textbooks. Our careers typically progress through a predictable series of decision points, each complete with a road map for the next several years and a bibliography of recommended reading. Stepping out of a clinical career path can open up an endless set of options with no road map – a seemingly daunting proposition for the physician mindset.

There is no textbook formula for pursuing a non-clinical career path. There is no test to take – no book ranking the jobs you are likely to encounter. Realizing the wide open possibilities following a departure from clinical practice can generate exhilaration, intimidation, or both.

As you begin to assess your particular non-clinical industry, try to identify any professional trade associations. Such organizations may have useful websites, allowing exposure to industry information, news, and journals. Reading through trade journals is a good way of learning whether the subject matter of the industry is of interest to you and provides a resource for identifying preferred companies and available positions.

In my case, while becoming increasingly interested in medical communications, I reviewed several trade journals, including *Med Ad News*,

Pharmaceutical Executive, *PharmaVOICE*, and *Medical Marketing & Media*. *Med Ad News* was particularly helpful in identifying numerous medical advertising agencies and targeting my search. I also joined the American Medical Writers Association, which has continued to be a helpful resource.

People, rather than standard research methods, are perhaps the best resource for learning about non-clinical job options. Career evolution often comes through keeping your eyes open for possibilities during all types of conversations. Opportunities follow through exploration and calculated risks.

Physicians open to such paradigm shifts in their behavior and thought process will find numerous potential paths to success.

QUESTION

Is there a list somewhere showing alternative career paths for physicians?

ANSWER

One of my biggest frustrations while exploring non-clinical career paths and searching for a new job was that I was unable to find a resource with comprehensive information on the subject. Unfortunately, there was no web site for physicians exploring non-clinical options across the spectrum of potential industries. The best I could do was track down small pockets of information. It was a terribly inefficient process just to locate these fragments. Then to regularly track updates from such sources was even more time consuming. I frequently went to the human resources pages of pharmaceutical company web sites and spent many evenings digging through postings on general job search web sites. Unfortunately, such listings tend to be reasonably helpful if you are seeking a specific position, but much less helpful if you are still in an exploration phase of your career transition.

During my non-clinical exploration, I was constantly in search of a one-stop resource. I knew what I wanted:

- A place where I could explore all of my options, rather than be restricted to an individual industry approach
- Information on the types of jobs that a physician could have within these industries
- Human resources web pages and job search lists at my fingertips

- Examples of physicians who were successful in making a similar career transition so that I could learn from their experience
- Tips on the career transition process
- Career enhancement information
- Links to graduate school programs, seminars, and industry information
- Access to individuals in my target industries

Since I could not find a web site that provided this information, I decided to create one for physicians like me. Physician Renaissance Network provides a comprehensive resource for doctors with non-clinical careers and interests. The web site (www.prnresource.com) is tailored to meet the needs of physicians who are considering a career transition or who are already in a non-clinical job and wish to enhance their industry expertise.

QUESTION

What job titles are the ones for physicians?

ANSWER

I am not sure why I stumbled through this issue while searching for jobs. I suppose it was because I never asked the right question, or maybe just never found the right answer anywhere. Part of the problem, of course, is that there was no single resource that spanned the different types of non-clinical jobs, and the position titles do vary across industries.

While there are no absolute rules, hierarchy in the workplace often progresses through the following titles: Associate (Assistant) Manager, Manager, Senior Manager, Associate (Assistant) Director, Director, Senior Director, Executive Director, Vice President, Senior Vice President, Executive Vice President, and President. Many companies have a Chief Scientific Officer or Chief Medical Officer position, usually at the Vice President or President level.

In my experience, it appears to be less likely for a physician to transition from clinical practice directly into a position higher than a Director level. Such thresholds vary according to numerous factors, however, including expertise, demand, and especially the size of the company, with smaller companies often offering higher titles.

Most physicians are familiar with titles in university and hospital administration settings, but what about the others? While this may sound obvious, the majority of medical positions have the word "Medical" in the job title. Medical Director is a common title across industries, as are those including the words "Medical Affairs."

When in doubt, check the education requirements, which are typically listed in a job posting. Jobs most suited to a physician's expertise will usually list a medical degree as either mandatory or beneficial. These positions also often pay more than similar sounding ones that do not require a medical degree.

QUESTION

How much money can a physician make in a non-clinical job?

ANSWER

This is as hard to answer as the question "How much does a physician make in a clinical job?" Think about all the factors that affect income in clinical practice: specialty, location, solo vs group, partnership vs employee, independent vs hospital-owned, private practice vs university setting, duration in one location, insurance mix, referral base, call schedule, willingness to work extra hours, luck, and so on. Salaries across all job types are influenced by external forces but also highly driven by individual factors. Where does salary fit on an individual's priority list? What in their life are they willing to give up for a high salary? How hard are they willing to work for it? After that, there is no question that a little bit of luck plays a role.

In the end, the potential salary and overall financial compensation depend on the value the individual provides and how much the employer and the market are willing to pay. Many physicians consider but then reject non-clinical options for financial reasons. Practitioners may complain about earning less than in the past, or less than their physician predecessors. What they often forget, however, is that despite the changes in modern medicine, physicians are still generally toward the top of the earning pyramid. While in practice, they provide a valuable service in areas of high demand. They have invested time in college, medical school, training, and clinical practice in order to achieve this high level of expertise.

Physicians transitioning to a non-clinical job bring with them a certain level of expertise, but still enter at the ground level in many cases. It is probably fairly difficult to imagine a cardiologist making more money as a new member of a marketing team than as an established clinician.

What about the earning potential over time? There are physicians who left clinical practice to work as volunteers, and others who made millions and retired young. Most non-clinical physicians who I know earn an annual base salary of $90,000 to $250,000. Compensation often extends beyond these base salary numbers and may include a bonus or commission, as well as additional benefits.

QUESTION

What was your most effective method of exploring your options?

ANSWER

Networking was, by far, the most efficient and effective way of researching and assessing my options. Other resources such as online information and trade journals definitely helped fill in the gaps, but nothing moved me forward faster than good old fashioned word of mouth.

Networking involves a combination or common sense and art, and can only be improved through practice. Physicians considering a non-clinical career transition frequently ask me about networking, so I have dedicated the next section of the book to this topic.

NETWORKING

QUESTION
How did you network?

ANSWER

My networking goals evolved over the two-year course of my job search. In the beginning I was networking mainly to talk to people who had general knowledge in relevant industries to research what types of options were out there. As time went on, I networked more to learn about specific companies and to identify available positions. From that point, speaking directly with the decision-makers who filled such positions became more important.

I spoke to most people over the telephone and took copious notes. I asked about their company and the types of jobs performed by physicians. I asked about their jobs and what their roles were in the company. I got a good sense of what each person liked and disliked about their position and how such a job would match my priority list. We also discussed potential career tracks for various jobs.

Before each conversation ended, I always asked if there were two or three other people that they would recommend having me call. I tried to get the contact information for those people before hanging up, and asked if they would be able to inform that person that I would be contacting them as a means of introduction. After the call I updated my contact list with any new information from the call, including the additional names that they identified. I also kept a second hand-drawn figure similar to a family tree showing which people had put me in touch with others. I continued to do this as my networking list expanded.

In the beginning I was only contacting one or two people every couple of weeks, but eventually I reached the point of making a few calls each day. Many of the people on the networking list were physicians working in the types of positions I was seeking; however, I was willing to talk to just about anyone recommended as someone who might be helpful in my search. There was no harm in speaking to anyone in these other industries, and I always felt as though the most important piece of information and a potential job were no more than one or two degrees of separation from the person I was calling on any given day.

Figure 6. Networking Process

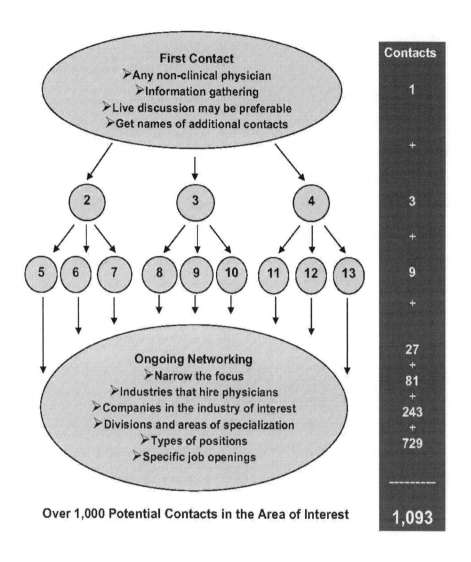

QUESTION

How did you start networking?

ANSWER

I made a list of everyone that I knew fairly well who had gone directly from my medical school class into the pharmaceutical industry. After hours of thinking about this, I had two names. One was a friend I had not seen since medical school. I tried to track him down through old contact information and common friends, but I was unsuccessful at doing that. This left me with only one name on my list, another good friend with whom I had maintained contact intermittently over the years. I felt embarrassed taking up his time talking about my career, but he was eager to help and informed me about numerous potential job positions within pharmaceuticals and several other related industries. He put me in touch with several people and gave me names of a few industry journals to review.

During that call I started asking him if there were any available positions in his company, but he gave me wise advice to spend some time researching my options in general and then hone in on a potential position once I decided what I wanted to do. This was somewhat difficult for me to accept at the time because after finally deciding to leave clinical practice, I was very eager to complete the transition. I conceded and heeded his advice.

By the end of the first call my networking list had grown to six people – six times the size of the original list. My networking process was underway. I now had new contacts across multiple industries. Each name would expand into its own network branch as long as I could propagate the series of new contact recommendations.

One of the people I eventually contacted put me in touch with several colleagues across multiple divisions in his pharmaceutical company, which provided a thorough download of how the industry worked and what the potential roles were for a physician. This networking process found its way into many corners of the company, and I eventually spoke to a large number of people.

This particular networking circle was helpful for a number of reasons. I was able to get 360-degree perspectives on individual positions. I also gradually learned that several of the types of positions that I had been pursuing through pharmaceutical company human resources web sites were either not aligned with my medical background or no longer appealing to me. I also learned that my interest within a pharmaceutical company would be in commercialization and marketing, rather than in research and development. As I look back now, this information seems obvious to me. At the time, however, I had no other way of knowing this information without these networking discussions.

One of the interesting things that happened during the course of this particular networking process was that I was invited to join my original contact and his colleagues in a men's hockey league game. I accepted the invitation and felt this would be a lot of fun, but also a great opportunity to meet more contacts in the company. Instead, what I learned was that a large number of the people from this pharmaceutical company had played college hockey and were able to skate circles around me. I generally found myself too out of breath to have any discussions about job opportunities at the company and was so far outplayed by the rest of the team that returning for another visit would have been pushing it a bit.

Overall, I found myself following two different networking patterns, without ever intending for that to be the case. One pattern was more expansive and allowed me to learn information across multiple industries. The other was more contained but allowed me to fully dissect the workings and potential positions available within a single large pharmaceutical company. Both were informative in different ways.

QUESTION

Was it tough to get people to talk to you?

ANSWER

I have always considered myself to be more of an introvert than an extrovert. I have also never felt comfortable asking people for help. As a result, the entire concept of networking was completely foreign to me. I remember feeling uncomfortable, even when talking to my friend who helped start the networking process. Calling strangers, introducing myself, and then asking for their time was particularly awkward. I realized; however, that I would not be able to accomplish what I needed to without such networking calls; pure necessity drove me past my inhibitions.

I was pleasantly surprised and increasingly grateful that nearly everyone I called was very willing to help. At the time it was difficult to understand why, because I felt as though I was impinging on their time. Now that I am frequently on the other side of those telephone calls, I can understand why people were so willing to help me. Talking on the phone is an easy thing to do and actually provides a short break from the more typical tasks of the day. Being able to help someone, especially if you can empathize with them, provides a great deal of satisfaction.

Some practicing physicians contemplating a career transition have expressed concern about the reactions they might get from people in positions that they desired. Was it possible that the people they would be calling would behave competitively and be reluctant to help someone who could later place their own job

73

security in jeopardy? This is actually a fairly naïve concern. Someone with experience in a particular position that is currently working in that job would not feel threatened by another individual with no experience at that job. It is the equivalent of a seasoned attending being intimidated by a medical student. In general, people seem flattered when called for advice or assistance and very eager to help.

QUESTION

What are some techniques to get people to talk to you?

ANSWER

People want to help each other – even the most impatient ones. If you can believe this, you can be successful networking. All you need to add is a combination of perseverance and consideration for the person you are contacting.

When contacting someone that you do not know, it is helpful to have the person referring you to the individual facilitate the introduction. When you then initiate contact it is extremely important to be respectful of that person's time and cater to their schedule.

Figure 7. Networking Communication

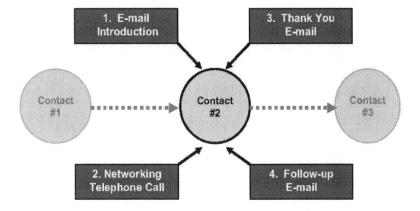

Sending a brief introductory e-mail is helpful. I usually mentioned the person who referred me and the objective for the call. I noted that I would be calling them within the next few days and that I would be happy to accommodate their schedule if there were particular days and times that worked best for them. I specified the amount of time that I would like to speak to them, usually 15 to 30 minutes. I obviously appreciated any opportunity to talk longer and found that most people were willing to do that.

During my telephone introduction I reminded them who referred me. I was always honest about how I knew the person, even if it was only through another networking call. People run out of patience if you start the conversation by overstating your relationship with the referring person. Always ask if you have called at a good time or whether they would prefer to schedule a later time. If people pick up the phone, they usually have a few minutes to talk and would prefer having a conversation at that time, rather than trying to reschedule.

Having some information about the person you are calling may prove helpful, especially when you can establish some common links. Do not be shy about asking for such information from the person referring you. A common *alma mater* can go a long way. Even a seemingly less significant link, such as my example of playing hockey, can help.

Another important step in networking is the follow-up. The common courtesy of a "thank you" email provides the added benefits of maintaining a connection with the individual and supporting the reputation of the person who originally made the referral for you. Reaching back to the original referring individual keeps them informed, provides them with the satisfaction of knowing they were able to help, and maintains an open line of communication for future contact during later phases of the networking process.

QUESTION

What questions did you ask during a networking call?

ANSWER

I always had a general agenda in mind for each networking call, along with specific objectives that I wanted to achieve. I made a list of questions before the call, in order to be as focused and efficient as possible. Some people that I contacted liked to talk, making conversation easy. Others gave yes/no answers; without a list of questions, these calls could end within a minute or two. Once I had someone on the line, I wanted to make sure that I could gain as much information from them within the allowed time.

The types of questions I asked on a networking call evolved over time. Initially I started with a more general approach. As I honed in on one industry and then particular positions, my questions became more specific.

Physicians in the types of positions that I was considering were a particularly great resource for me to ask as many questions as possible. What was the job title? What were the original entry level position, the progression since then, and a typical career track for the future? In what area of the company was the position? What was the overall reporting structure of that area? What were the general functions of the job? What was a typical day like? With what other team members did this particular position interact? What did they like about their position? What did they dislike? Was there a lot of travel involved? Were the day-to-day interactions limited to a certain department, extend throughout the company, or reach outside to individuals such as other physicians?

There were other questions about the company. Was this type of position available at other companies? What was unique about the position within this particular company? What was it like to work for the company? What other types of positions were available for physicians there? I would then run through a similar list of questions regarding those positions. Would they recommend speaking with someone in those other positions at their company? Were there currently any open positions for physicians?

During the course of the discussion I would try to learn about the person's background and how they got into this particular job. Most people had held other positions in their current company, another company in the industry, or a different industry altogether. They taught me about many opportunities for physicians, as well as specific types of positions that would be the best options for a physician making a career transition. I tried to get a sense of whether their current position was the type that someone with limited or no specific experience would be able to do. Usually this was not the case.

I always asked for a few recommendations of other people to contact. I asked if they would mind my using their name, or even provide a brief introduction through email. I tried to learn a little about these next networking contacts and always made sure to get their telephone number and/or email address before hanging up.

QUESTION

Who did you contact to network?

ANSWER

I was willing to talk to almost anybody who was in one of the industries I was considering. Obviously, I primarily tried to speak with physicians. I also found it very helpful to talk to people who were not in the positions that I was considering but interacted with them, so that I could better understand a new perspective on the position. From a networking standpoint, I learned that even if I was speaking with someone who was not one of my primary targets, they were often an important link to another person who was.

In general, these non-clinical physicians enjoyed their jobs. They were also candid regarding the negative aspects of the job. Along the way, I learned from these people what it was like to work in their position and also why they chose not to do other particular jobs available to physicians. Sometimes I heard contrasting opinions back-to-back, which allowed me to make my own assessment based on multiple perspectives.

Over time, as I honed in on my options, I gained a thorough understanding of the types of positions that I was considering.

QUESTION

Did you get any support from your *alma maters* or the hospital programs where you trained?

ANSWER

The alumni offices were helpful; I highly recommend contacting them.

I visited my college alumni web site and found a mentoring program that I could join. For about $25, I got a list of numerous individuals in different professions who were willing to answer questions and provide networking support. I contacted a few of these people, and all provided helpful advice. One gentleman who worked for a large pharmaceutical company was particularly helpful and launched me into the extensive networking circle within his company that I mentioned previously.

My medical school alumni office provided contact information for individuals that I wanted to contact, but did not have an established networking process to suit my needs. I am currently teaming up with other alumni from my medical school to recommend networking efforts specifically focused toward non-clinical careers.

Training programs are not geared toward the types of jobs that I was considering, so I did not go to them for help. I later found that my professors had little knowledge about my current industry, and some cases were even opposed to my transition. Other job types may be better suited to recommendations from training program physicians.

PREPARATION

QUESTION

How can I make a career transition when I have no skills for another job?

ANSWER

It is very important to look at the realistic chances of being able to transition into a specific job. I believe that it is possible to reach almost any job from another. That is not to say that I considered NFL quarterback on my list of possibilities when I started my search. But beyond the unfathomable, the vast majority of jobs are somewhere within reach. The question usually is whether or not you are willing to pay the price to get there. If you lack a certain certification or skill set, it is possible that gaining that expertise may be too time-consuming or expensive to be worthwhile.

Physicians considering alternative career paths often immediately equate "expertise" with their specific type of training, and focus on the clinical component of their day-to-day work. I did this at first. I was very skilled at plastic surgery and hand surgery and knew that I would not be doing either of those two activities in a new job. I thought that all I knew how to do was operate. As I began to interview, and especially after I announced my career transition, many people asked why I was throwing away all of those years of training for a completely different job.

The typical clinical career path of physicians relies heavily upon formalized training, which we consequently identify as a determinant of "experience." If physicians have no formal training in marketing, sales, business development, or people management, they mistakenly feel as though they have no experience in these subjects. What they do not realize, however, is that the vast majority of successful leaders in the other industries that they are considering also lack such formal training; they have generally learned these skills "on the job." Practicing clinicians have acquired many of the same skills as individuals in other types of industries; they simply have not noticed the educational process occurring.

When I went back and assessed the skills that I gained in my practice, I realized many of these were actually ideally suited to jobs in other industries. This became particularly obvious to me after I began interviewing. I was often asked if I had any experience in managing people. At first I would answer "no", but after time I realized I had a great deal of experience managing people. As a chief resident in plastic surgery, I managed teams of varying experience levels, from students to senior residents. Being a surgeon in an operating room requires a great deal of management experience to coordinate the efforts of the surgical assistants, nurses and other personnel. For years I managed people in such settings where the consequences of poor results meant loss of function or loss of life for the patient. Managing people under high risk conditions required a unique level of composure and confidence that would be beneficial in any setting.

Chances are that you have the skills necessary to perform many other types of jobs, and that you would not be throwing away your experience prior to the career transition – only building upon it. Perhaps negative thinking is the only obstacle between you and a successful career transition. Physicians generally downplay their experience and contributions; successfully transitioning careers requires a different and perhaps even uncomfortable approach to self-commercialization. The necessary skills are most likely there in some form or fashion; packaging and selling them is the next step.

QUESTION

What skills transfer well to a non-clinical job?

ANSWER

Physicians have several skills that are broadly applicable across other industries.

Managing a practice is in many ways similar to operating a small company. The clinical issues of patient care are only the tip of the iceberg. People management in clinical practice goes far beyond telling a nurse that the patient in the examining room needs their leg wrapped in gauze. There are decisions regarding hiring, firing, and raises. Employees need education, training, and career development. Human resource issues sometimes arise. Physicians manage or interact with the process of financial matters, such as accounts receivable, accounts billable, payroll, employee benefits, and office supply inventory.

A typical day in the physician's office requires several other skill sets. Physicians are particularly good at multi-tasking and have to meet frequent deadlines with regard to treatment decisions and ancillary paperwork. Interacting with patients requires a great deal of interpersonal skill, one-on-one conversation, education, psychological assessment, and sometimes even mind-reading. Good physicians are bright people, fast learners, and even better listeners. Few groups of people have better problem solving skills. Physicians are often good writers, a benefit in most types of jobs.

Many physicians are good public speakers, a characteristic commonly sought by managers. Speaking at meetings and new business pitches can bring revenue to the company and open opportunities for the individual.

Physicians have an ability to deal with stress that far exceeds the average human being. Whenever my work seems stressful, I imagine the week when I spent 156 hours in the hospital working in the Open Heart Recovery Room. There is nothing that a non-clinical job can throw at a physician that is tougher than the easiest day in internship. My stamina and composure in the workplace are partly due to the fact that I have survived residency training.

A lot of these characteristics have become so second nature to physicians that they dismiss them as being fairly typical of the average person. It is important before an interview to take an assessment of these characteristics and think through how you will want to convey them in a cohesive and believable story. Do not take them for granted. Communicating this correctly may be a key factor in getting a new type of job.

QUESTION

How can I "beef up" my resume?

ANSWER

Addressing this question leads to an age-old challenge in the workplace: How can you get a job without having experience, and how can you get the experience without having a job?

Strengthening your resume requires taking a close look at the job description and specific requirements for the position that you are considering. When researching Medical Director positions within the medical communications industry, I realized that writing skills differentiated candidates. I searched my files and gathered the samples of my writing from the last several years. This included a short story, several scientific and clinical articles in medical journals, and some editorials in a plastic surgery journal. I made sure that this writing experience was detailed and prominently featured on my resume. Realizing that it could take several months or even longer to make a career transition, I made a plan to gain additional writing experience during this period in order to strengthen my skills and resume.

I sent emails to numerous medical web sites, submitting information about my background and expressing an interest in writing. The larger companies had established writing staff and did not respond. As a result, I ended up mainly writing for two lesser known but professionally managed web sites, www.personalmd.com and www.suite101.com. I wrote nearly 20 web-based articles during that year. These created a nice online writing portfolio where potential employers could easily view my work.

I began seeking freelance writing opportunities through several online postings and the American Medical Writers Association newsletter shortly before my job offer came through. Although I did not end up doing any freelance work myself, this is something that I frequently recommend to people who are considering writing in the medical communications industry. Freelancing could improve the productivity and quality of your writing and serve as a testing ground for your targeted job.

While my personal experience is in medical communications, freelance opportunities are not unique to this industry. There are ways to pick up project work or provide consulting services across numerous areas, including the pharmaceutical, legal, and medical publishing industries, just to name a few.

A physician may be able to increase freelance volume in a step-wise fashion, potentially converting from full-time to part-time clinical practice and then completing the transition to a new job. Alternatively, if the fit is not desirable, then the physician has not burned any bridges and can continue clinical practice full-time while investigating alternative options. Similarly, freelance projects allow potential employers to interact with you, assess your work, and evaluate you for future positions.

There are as many ways to gain additional education, training, or certification as there are jobs. Some physicians choose to obtain advanced degrees such as a Master of Public Health (MPH) or Master of Business Administration (MBA). Others prefer to take individual courses to fill specific educational gaps, rather than making the full time commitment required for a degree.

Professional organizations within certain industries provide education and networking opportunities. In addition, membership in such organizations may reflect additional interest and commitment to the industry when viewed on a resume. When I was looking for Medical Writer and Medical Director positions, I joined the American Medical Writers Association, which sends out a monthly newsletter with postings for available jobs and freelance opportunities, as well as information on applicants looking for such positions. Members also have access to a quarterly journal, numerous networking opportunities through local chapters, and an annual meeting.

QUESTION
Should I get an MBA?

ANSWER

Nearly every physician in clinical practice who is considering a career transition asks me if they should get a Master of Business Administration (MBA) degree. It is difficult not to answer with another question: "What do you hope to accomplish with the MBA?"

Becoming a physician requires well-defined graduate school education. In fact, practicing physicians have all completed training programs, and many have finished specialty fellowships or even sub-specialty fellowships. This background often leaves the misperception that optimal success in any job requires a well-defined and regimented education process. Another common misperception is that having an MBA will make someone more successful in business than they would be without the degree.

Getting an MBA is a substantial time commitment. The education generally requires two years of full-time study. There are now many executive MBA program options that allow flexible options or part-time study over a longer period in order to gain the full education to earn the degree. These can become particularly taxing, usurping weekends and spare time.

Another consideration is whether pursuing this education will limit or eliminate your earning potential while matriculating. This financial commitment needs to be weighed against the potential but often unpredictable amount of financial benefit to going to business school.

Despite these caveats, however, there may be quite compelling reasons to include business school as part of a career transition process. People often talk about "getting an MBA," which suggests that the important part of the process is having three letters attached to the end of your name on your resume. While there is often some degree of benefit associated with having the degree on your credential list, it is outweighed by the value of the knowledge gained from attending business school. For this reason, *where* to go to business school is just as important as *whether* to go.

A good friend of mine demonstrated very well how going to business school can be an important component of a well thought out career transition plan. He had been an emergency room physician for many years and for various reasons decided to work toward a job in hospital administration. While still juggling full-time shifts in the emergency room, he was able to attend Columbia University's Executive MBA Program. His goal was to take on an administrative position in his hospital and then gradually work his way up to a Chief Executive Officer or Chief Operating Officer position. In speaking to numerous people in the hospital system he learned that having an MBA was an unwritten job requirement necessary to reach that level, from both credential and knowledge standpoints.

The educational experience that he had at Columbia was very rewarding and yet quite challenging. He rarely had weekends or much spare time to himself and his family during the three years of his business school education. During the time he was in business school; however, he transitioned from his clinical emergency room shifts to a full-time hospital administration position. He has since risen to a Vice President position, finds his work extremely rewarding, and uses his business school knowledge every day. He feels that business school was time, effort and money well spent in order to make the transition that he was seeking. He is an example of someone who laid out a plan, an important component of which was going to business school. If you have this type of well thought out reason for "getting an MBA," then the additional education may be ideally suited to your needs.

QUESTION

Did you consider getting an MBA?

ANSWER

Yes, there were times during my career transition when I considered going to business school. The information gained from such education would be helpful in many positions in business. In my case, the education probably would have helped in a more general way, rather than advancing my career through specific promotion opportunities. When I evaluated business school as a potential option, I decided that the potential benefit would not be worth the financial or time commitment.

From speaking to people who have gone to business school midstream in their careers, there appear to be several benefits to the experience. One reason is that business school provides an organized structure within which you can read adequately on the necessary topics. I set up a business-focused reading list for myself a couple of times in the past and have found it a challenge to complete the "assignments" in my spare time. Having the structure of business school classes, the threat of exams, and the dedicated time to do this reading would be beneficial.

The lectures provided by business school professors are difficult to reproduce outside of the classroom. Some of the top business schools within driving distance of my home provide week-long and month-long executive courses focused on specific topics, several of which interested me as I reached a management position. Some companies reimburse their employees for taking such courses. My company did not, and I chose not to attend any of these courses, again due to the cost and time commitment necessary.

Another benefit touted by people who have gone to business school is the ability to learn from your peers. Business schools attract students with widely varying backgrounds, including expertise from different industries and positions. Students share their experiences and interact, especially when working through case studies and business plans.

I worked in a $50 billion company that acquired numerous smaller entities. As a result, my division was led by a senior management team composed of entrepreneurs. Recognizing this unique situation, I set out to learn as much as possible from these managers.

I identified several business skills in which I was deficient and tried to address these gaps with my manager and other individuals with expertise to share. Finance and accounting were two such areas. Over time I learned how to navigate through and prepare standard spreadsheets. What I could not pick up from meetings with my managers, I supplemented through discussions with relatives who owned businesses.

I was also fortunate to be selected among a handful of individuals to participate in a corporate-wide "Mentoring Leaders Program." My mentor was president of another division in the company; together we set up my training agenda. He developed an easily achievable but very informative reading curriculum. Every few weeks, we discussed the key points of the books and ways to apply their lessons to the department that I was managing. This was a unique learning experience that helped me a great deal.

Overall, I treated my management experience as on-the-job business education and feel I benefited a great deal from this approach. In some ways this was an inadequate substitution for business school, but in other ways it was far superior. Most importantly, this plan helped me achieve my objectives.

QUESTION

Should I become board certified before my career transition?

ANSWER

I was recently asked by a resident one year from completing his psychiatry residency whether he should move to a non-clinical job right away, or finish his training and become board certified first. The answer to this question is obviously complex, multi-faceted and highly individualized. In the pharmaceutical industry and in my area of medical communications, I feel it would be very helpful for such an individual to become board certified in a specialty such as psychiatry, which is in high demand. Other factors are involved in the cost/benefit assessment for this person when considering the additional time, effort and money necessary to achieve board certification. My personal feeling is that once you are that close, you should finish. Completing a training program and/or obtaining board certification has potential benefits in a new job, provides peer recognition and a sense of accomplishment, and probably most importantly, permits the flexibility to practice part-time or even return to practice in the future.

ACQUISITION

QUESTION
How did you find your job?

ANSWER

It took two years of hard work and optimism to make it through to the other side of the search process. Interestingly, my search concluded with what I consider to be a true stroke of luck. Without the first 99% of hard work, however, I would not have been in a position to benefit from luck, and to recognize the opportunity when it was within my grasp.

Through researching and networking, I decided to enter medical communications. Then a physician working in a pharmaceutical company told me about a trade publication called *Med Ad News,* which publishes an annual report of the top medical communications companies. He even pointed me to the specific issue that had this listing. I went to my hospital's medical library, photocopied the entire issue, and reviewed the detailed descriptions of about 100 medical communications companies.

I live in Bethlehem, Pennsylvania, just outside of New Jersey, a major hub for much of this industry. As a result, I was able to identify about 50 medical communication companies within a 75-mile radius of my home. I then drafted a letter introducing myself, talking about my background, and then describing why I wanted to transition to medical communications. I mailed a pile of letters to the contact people listed in *Med Ad News*.

Unsolicited introductory letters are generally considered to be a low-yield technique of job searching. The odds of finding a company looking to hire, especially for a position that matches your expertise, are quite low. In addition, a known entity is traditionally a better hire than an unknown person writing a cold-call letter.

In my positions since leaving practice I cannot recall hiring someone following receipt of a cold-call letter. That is not to say that I dismiss such letters. It is more likely that we were just not looking for such expertise at the time. We currently respond to unsolicited letters, at least with an email or phone call to acknowledge receipt. If the person has the expertise that we need, we start with a telephone screening or go straight to an interview. In some cases, if the candidate ideally matches our general hiring specifications but contacts us during a period when no positions are available, we might even bring them in for an exploratory interview for future positions. In addition, I take special interest in being able to speak with physicians who reach out to us, in some cases as a screening for future positions, but more often to provide some general guidance in their search process. We keep such communication on file for future consideration.

Following my letter writing campaign, I heard back from one company months later – long after giving up hope for any responses. They had an opening for a Medical Director at the time. The series of interviews that followed went well, but I did not get that position. In retrospect, I think that my salary requirements exceeded the benefit that my expertise would have brought to that specific position. A few months later; however, the same company contacted me for a more junior Associate Medical Director position. They had just gotten an account for a bioengineered skin product that was being marketed to plastic surgeons. In this case, my plastic surgery expertise was perfectly aligned with the product account, creating an ideal fit for me, the employer, and the client.

I accepted this job and made the transition to medical communications.

QUESTION

Did you find on-line job listings useful?

ANSWER

I did not find them to be useful, mostly because I could not locate non-clinical physician job postings in a single place. Variation in job title designation also made the process confusing, and at times maddening. I found myself digging for hours on general job search sites, only to find one or two possibilities that were in the general realm of what I was seeking.

There are scattered web sites that list open positions for specific types of companies that would be of interest to physicians. It is important to note the posting date, however, since some of these positions will already be filled by the time you see them.

I applied electronically for a few jobs posted on pharmaceutical company websites but never even received confirmation that the applications were received. Had I been aggressively pursuing these particular jobs, I would have tracked down the appropriate person to follow up, but that was not the case.

Unfortunately, at the time of my search, there was no comprehensive resource specifically addressing the needs of physicians interested in making a career transition.

QUESTION

What makes a company want to hire a physician?

ANSWER

The complete answer to this question obviously depends upon the specific job, but there are a few common threads. Some positions require the knowledge obtained through a medical doctorate. Others require clinical experience. A broad clinical background is sometimes best to allow work across multiple therapeutic categories. In other cases, such as with particular pharmaceuticals, it is best to have a physician on staff with specific expertise in the product's therapeutic area.

From an employer standpoint, hiring a physician generally requires a relatively high salary. Increasing specialty expertise requirements will usually inflate the salary, as well as the overall compensation associated with bonuses and the benefits package. As a result, if a position can be done just as well by a non-physician, then a company would probably prefer not to hire a physician for that position. Similarly, if being a physician is beneficial for a position, but specific therapeutic expertise is not necessary, then a candidate's specialty experience may not equate to additional market value and salary. The employer has to go through a cost/benefit assessment of the physician's worth, in order to weigh the marginal value of additional expertise against higher salary requirements.

Another important question is whether an employer views a physician transitioning from clinical practice as a viable hiring option in comparison to someone who has already been working in the industry.

All other things being equal, a physician who has experience at a certain type of industry position is generally a better choice than one who does not. Many physicians contemplating a career transition seem to underestimate the importance of this distinction and assume that they can jump into a new industry as an expert. To best illustrate the point, consider whether you would rather be treated in July by a new intern or an attending who has been practicing for several years.

Before the thought of returning to the level of a first-day intern becomes too demoralizing, keep in mind that many factors go into the decision of which candidate to hire. Employers are often willing to work with a practicing physician who appears to be a good candidate and help train them, as long as there is a potential fit from an expertise and personality standpoint. Keep in mind, however, that if a job description lists a mandatory number of years' experience within that type of position, it is unlikely that someone making a career transition will get that particular job. Even if such a candidate squeaks through the application process, there is a good chance that they will be over their head and quickly dissatisfied. A discussion with a potential employer as to whether such experience is mandatory or simply a "nice to have" recommendation may help clarify this.

QUESTION

I have decided that I like a certain type of job. What do I do next?

ANSWER

It is crucial to thoroughly assess the type of position that you are considering.

The first check on the position that you are considering should be to score it on the priority list that you set up earlier in the search process. This position should score higher than your current one. Keep in mind that your priorities as you originally listed them may have changed a little bit during the course of the search process. No need to worry; that is a normal occurrence. What you need to avoid, however, is force-fitting your priority list to match the job you are considering, simply because you want out of clinical practice. No job option will perfectly match up with your priorities, but the one you select should come pretty close.

It is important to be as objective as possible when assessing your qualifications for the job that you are considering. Some jobs require specific training and/or certification. Others require (or at least strongly prefer) a minimum amount of experience in a particular industry or position. This is an important time to have a reality check about your goals. Is the position that you want something that you can achieve with your current level of expertise, or will you require additional preparation to be a strong candidate?

In my current industry, medical communications, it is feasible to do freelance work. This option may help further assess whether this is the right career transition option for you. Freelancing may further assist in the networking process and help you identify a company where there is a mutual fit. Such experience will also bolster your resume and might even convince potential employers that you are capable of doing the job well.

Okay. Now you are certain about the particular type of position.

Next, map out a plan and a time course for making your career transition, including particular milestone goals along the way. If getting additional graduate school education is necessary, for example, you will need to decide whether this is something you want to do part-time, or whether you can afford to do it full-time.

Allow yourself enough time for the job search and interview process. You may get lucky and have this move along quickly, but it could easily take several months. Outlining the milestones for this process in advance can provide motivation to meet your deadlines along the way and minimize frustration over the search taking a long time.

The nature of your networking will probably change during this time. Backtracking through your networking lists can yield further specifics that you might not have asked during a preliminary call. With new and previous contacts, you can also be more certain in your conviction and inquire about potential job opportunities in their company. Networking further into particular companies that seemed promising to you along the course of your research may open the door for a job.

QUESTION

Is geography and willingness to relocate an issue?

ANSWER

In certain jobs these factors are influential, and in others they are not. You do not necessarily need to give up if the company or even the entire industry is located far away; working remotely may be an option. Physicians familiar with NightHawk Radiology Services, a company providing centralized reading centers in Switzerland and Australia, understand that the concept of working remotely has even found a successful home in the practice of medicine.

An acceptable position may be located close to home, but the ideal position may require relocation. Hospital administration jobs are available throughout the country, for example, but you may find that a particular type of administrative position in the university setting that you desire may be far away from your home. Similarly, a large number of public health jobs are available throughout the country, but if you are aiming for a particular position at the NIH, the CDC, or a federal government setting, you may be more limited in geographical options.

A large number of jobs in the insurance industry and in legal consulting exist throughout the country. Medical analyst positions within the financial sector tend to be in centralized pockets in major cities; however, there may also be the potential flexibility of working remotely as a consultant or even in a staff position.

The pharmaceutical industry in the United States has traditionally been heavily based in the Northeast, primarily between New York City and Philadelphia. Satellite industries, such as medical communications, have followed the geographical lead of the pharmaceutical companies. When exploring options in this field, I was fortunate to live very close to this area. There are other enlarging areas where this industry resides, however, such as Boston, Baltimore, Washington, D.C., Chicago, the research triangle in North Carolina, and pockets in northern and southern California. The enormous size of this industry also allows for opportunities in many other locations across the United States.

During the research process it is important to learn whether the position that you are considering can be done remotely from your home or with a part-time commuting option. I know a physician who splits his time between his home in Boston and a pharmaceutical company in Southern California, and a Vice President of Marketing who splits her time between her home in Arizona and a pharmaceutical company in New York. In such cases, the benefits of remaining in your existing home must be weighed against the inconvenience of frequent travel. In some cases, working off-site may also limit the chance of being promoted.

QUESTION

What should I emphasize in an introductory letter?

ANSWER

The introductory letter should emphasize three main questions:

1) Why are you interested in this industry/position?
2) Why are you interested in this particular company?
3) How does your background make you well suited for this position?

Why are you interested in this industry/position?

It is important that you describe why you are looking at this type of position. When an introductory letter does not clearly identify a position of interest, it demonstrates that the writer does not have a good understanding of the roles of medical professionals in this type of company.

Some applicants write letters mentioning several positions of interest. A list that includes unrelated jobs suggests a lack of understanding of the responsibilities and experience requirements involved. This may not seem like a big problem to an applicant who is not yet well versed in this new industry, but it is an obvious warning signal to a potential employer. The applicant will have a difficult time conveying a sincere desire to work in a particular position after making this mistake.

The best way to avoid this pitfall is to research the different types of positions within this type of company (ideally this particular company) and understand which are most suited to the applicant's background and interest.

Why are you interested in this particular company?

Employers, like anyone else, want to feel as though they have been selected above their competitors, rather than simply targeted in a "shotgun" application approach. Mentioning who recommended the company is generally helpful. You should have specific reasons for applying. Perhaps the company has expertise in a particular therapeutic area or is currently working with a client or product of interest to you. A mutual interest would provide the greatest likelihood of finding a match between you and the company.

How does your background make you well suited for this position?

As with other portions of the letter, this should come across as being sincere and not boastful. If you are applying for a Medical Director position working on an epilepsy product at a pharmaceutical company, you will obviously want to mention that you are a neurologist with extensive experience presenting and writing on the topic.

Overall it is important to keep the letter brief, limiting it to one or two paragraphs. Anything much longer than this will probably dilute the key points that you were trying to make and lose a busy reader halfway through. It is best to address the letter to a specific individual at the company who is an appropriate recipient of it. It is also extremely important to use a tone that conveys that you are eagerly pursuing a new job, rather than fleeing your current one.

The letter should include your personal contact information and preferred means of communication. An updated curriculum vitae (CV) or resume should be attached.

QUESTION

What should I emphasize in my resume/CV?

ANSWER

You should first check to see whether a CV or resume is more appropriate for your industry. A resume is much more succinct than the CVs that physicians typically prepare for clinical, faculty, or research positions. While either option is often acceptable for physicians applying for non-clinical jobs, I will focus the answer on resumes, which are more standard for my industry.

A well written resume needs to be fine tuned to highlight the pertinent points as they relate to the specific industry and position for which you are applying. If you are like me, your resume still contains certain lingering items that you find difficult to delete. Maybe the high school math club no longer needs to be there. Then again, maybe it does. This is the perfect time for you to reassess such items and try and streamline the overall flow of the resume. One of the best ways to do this is to have people who are involved in your industry of interest and/or who conduct interviews review your resume and provide constructive criticism.

Next, do your own review from the perspective of someone considering hiring you for that position. Consider the skill sets that will be important for the position and make sure to incorporate these in a succinct but noticeable way. Potential employers in this new industry will be viewing your resume in a different way than a hospital or a clinician considering hiring you for their staff. For example, you may now want to include the number of office staff that you manage. Similarly, you may want to add the fact that you presented to more than ten community patient groups over the course of the past year. The first example speaks to your management experience, and the second to your communication skills. As physicians, we often take such examples of our skill sets for granted because they have become second nature. Do not assume that a potential employer knows that you do such activities. Think about what you do every day at work, and you will undoubtedly find relevant information to include.

If you have an extensive number of publications or oral presentations or similar items listed in your standard resume, you may want to break these out to a separate appendix and simply write "see attached" within the main portion of the resume. This will allow the reviewer to focus on what they consider to be most relevant within the resume itself but still be impressed by the volume of the other items and be able to reference those if needed.

After editing the resume, you should again have a few extremely meticulous friends review it. Make sure that the organization and formatting are ideal and that there are no typographical errors. Until you get to an interview, the resume will do all the talking for you, so it should be flawless.

Do a final review from the standpoint of a potential employer with regard to a particular position. Identify any gaps in your background that would limit your ability to perform well in this job. You should then try to fill in these gaps with past examples or identify ways to enhance your expertise in these areas while undertaking the job search.

QUESTION

What do you want to see on a resume/CV?

ANSWER

This is obviously quite different for various positions. I will focus on applicants for Medical Director positions within medical communications since this is the area where I have the most experience as a manager.

There are two types of applicants that I consider. The first is someone we are considering for a very specific open position. The other is someone that we would like to meet as an "exploratory interview" with potential future positions in mind.

The specific open position is more straightforward. We do business across all major therapeutic areas. Oncology work requires very specific expertise. A generalist, either from clinical practice or from within our industry, is generally not adequately prepared for a position dealing with an oncology account. As a result, we would typically be looking for a Medical Director with an advanced scientific degree (eg, MD, PharmD, PhD) and at least several years of clinical and/or industry experience in oncology.

Even within oncology, more specific expertise is ideal. For example, someone with a fair amount of leukemia experience may not be the best person for work in a solid tumor category. There are other areas such as cardiology that are similarly demanding from a specific expertise standpoint. The subdivisions here are also very particular, such as expertise within hypertension, arrhythmias or anticoagulants. Certain central nervous system disorders are also demanding from a therapeutic expertise standpoint.

When a person will be working on multiple smaller accounts or a larger account in a less demanding therapeutic area, a more general background is acceptable and often even preferable. There are numerous advantages to having a broad therapeutic area experience in our industry. Accounts will change over time due to the fate of the individual product (eg, not achieving FDA approval, being recalled, going off patent, or experiencing budget cuts for other reasons) or changing relationships with a client. Someone with a broad background can more easily switch to another account or take on new products over time. This flexibility is important from a staffing and new business planning standpoint.

Writing skills and experience are generally important in our industry; I look for this in the resumes that I review. Most physicians have authored scientific or clinical publications. A complete lack of publications is a red flag for a writer or Medical Director candidate, and a large number is a plus. Prior editorial positions with journals or a creative writing hobby are also beneficial on a resume.

Communication skills are crucial. Usually this is difficult to ascertain on paper. Someone who lists a good number of prior presentations or experience in a position that requires a lot of client interaction promises to have good communication skills. This attribute usually comes across better later during the interview.

In medical communications our work has to be well organized and very meticulous. One easy way that I will sometimes dismiss potential candidates is through review of a poorly organized or otherwise sloppy resume. It is hard to convince someone that you are a good writer if your resume is poorly written.

QUESTION

Did you go through a recruiter?

ANSWER

I did not go through a recruiter to search for jobs, but the option is reasonable and one that I probably should have pursued.

There are recruiters who specialize in the types of positions that a clinical physician might be seeking. Most recruiters work on behalf of the employer to fill open positions. They generally do not work on behalf of an applicant to find such positions, although they keep contact information on file in case a suitable opportunity arises. I have utilized the services of recruiters in my management positions.

Recruiters generally specialize in certain job types within particular industries. Some are open to discussions with physicians in clinical practice who are considering a career transition; others find such candidates to be higher maintenance with a low likelihood of actually changing jobs in the end. Discussions with recruiters early in the search process are best used for educational purposes; moving right to a position search is getting the cart before the horse. Once you have identified the type of position that you are seeking, calls to reputable recruiters may prove beneficial.

It is difficult for an individual in practice to know which recruiters would be most helpful to their specific needs. Today, as I do a test search for recruiters on the internet, a number of web sites come up, but career types and specific positions are generally not listed. It is also difficult for someone with little knowledge in this area to know which recruiters are the most reputable within the industry, a factor that is important not just in identifying good opportunities, but in negotiating compensation and other benefits later in the process. Finding reputable recruiters should be part of the networking process.

How did interviewers react to your career transition?

I always assumed that interviewers were wondering if there was something wrong with me that explained my decision to leave clinical practice. After all, plastic surgery has the public image of being one of the least strenuous and most lucrative specialties in medicine. Why would someone leave all that?

Everyone that interviewed me asked the same question. They would start by saying, "I have to ask you . . . Why would you . . . " They were deciding how to finish the sentence. They either asked, "Why would you throw away all those years of training?" or "Why would you want to leave a plastic surgery practice?"

So, what were they thinking? *Maybe he had a nervous breakdown. Maybe he is an alcoholic. Maybe he had a ton of malpractice lawsuits.* What about this one? *Maybe he was simply not a good surgeon.*

One of my less timid interviewers quickly moved past such concerns by saying, "Listen, people have reasons for changing jobs. You seem like you will do well at this job. Just promise me you're not going to end up being a jerk." He did not actually use the word "jerk," but I think you get the picture. I took that job and the interviewer became one of my favorite bosses ever.

I suppose that it does not matter very much what interviewers think of your career transition, but rather how they think you will perform in the job.

QUESTION

What did you want to learn when you were interviewing for a job?

ANSWER

Before I went on an interview, I did a significant amount of research into the industry that I was considering. I visited the web site of the company where I was interviewing and learned as much as possible from additional reading and networking resources.

During the interview process, I asked about the overall structure of the company and the reporting structure for my desired position. I tried to get a sense of a typical career path for a person starting in that position. Learning as much as possible about the management style and business philosophy of the company was important. I wanted a better understanding of the working environment and the team dynamic.

I looked for a sense of stability. Information regarding recent account wins and losses, as well as future growth potential, was important in this regard. Understanding the company's approach to new business development and growth was helpful. When speaking with peer-level interviewers, I asked about past trends regarding the size of the staff, especially the medical team. Sometimes this can lead to discussions about prior rounds of layoffs, or people in your position who have recently resigned.

I wanted to learn about the day-to-day activities and interactions of the position. Again, certain questions were asked of management, and others of peer-level interviewers. I asked about my anticipated account(s), how the teams were structured, and who the key individuals were on those teams. The specifics about the account projects were helpful to know. I wanted a general sense of my daily interactions, both internally and externally. In the case of Medical Director positions within medical communications, I was interested in how much interaction I would have with clients and outside physicians.

When interviewing with someone working in a similar position, I would ask them to walk me through a typical day. Through this discussion I could learn about their workload and how much travel they had to do, without specifically asking such questions that suggested I was not willing to work hard. What they liked and disliked most about the position would generally come through.

There is an art to discussing financial compensation during a telephone screening and live interviews. Early on in my search, I wanted to find out right away what the salary and overall compensation were. I felt as though I might be wasting my time without getting to this important point right away. Initially this was okay because I was targeting positions that were inappropriate for my medical background and far below my salary requirements. Once I began targeting the right types of positions, however, I realized the main goal of the first few discussions was to sell the company on my expertise and ability to do the job. This approach may seem inefficient, but it avoids prematurely shutting the door on an opportunity by discussing salary too early. There is generally at least some degree of expectation that physicians will be demanding with their salary requirements, so employers will quickly end discussions when this red flag is raised. If you are employed as a clinician and earning a higher salary than that offered in the new position that you are considering, which is common and was the case for me, then you have the time to negotiate the compensation package.

Overall, I see the interview as a conversation to assess whether there is a mutual fit. It is just as important for me to decide whether I would be happy with the company as it is to convince the company that they should hire me. Obviously, both sides have to be happy in the end.

QUESTION

What do you look for when interviewing an applicant?

ANSWER

Meeting with an applicant is time consuming, so we are relatively selective during the initial resume and telephone screening process. By the time someone comes in for an interview, they have met several criteria that can be assessed on a piece of paper, and their education and work background have exceeded the threshold for the position. The interview is a chance to determine whether the applicant has the traits necessary to excel at the position.

I approach an interview from either direction as a conversation. As an employer my goals are to convince the applicant that our company is the best place to work, but then also to assess whether they would be a good fit for the position under discussion. I usually get clarification on a few specific questions that I have about their background. After that, the main goal is to assess whether the applicant will meet the expectations of several important people: their manager, the account team(s), the client(s), and me.

Applicants must have the ability to listen. The way that someone interacts during an interview, when on their best behavior, is indicative of the best communication skills that they will exhibit later when speaking with their account team or a client. The inability to listen causes interpersonal issues, misdirection, inefficiency, increased expense, and therefore a threat to business. Too many job candidates come in like a hurricane, trying to tell you

129

everything on their checklist, rather than holding a conversation and listening to what the interviewer has to say. As a result, they end up missing the opportunity to learn about the interviewer and the company, and they may make a bad impression.

A candidate has to show a level of enthusiasm about the position for which they are applying. Most importantly, they should be at the interview because they are excited about moving toward something, rather than escaping a negative past experience. This is particularly true for physicians who are considering a career transition. Sometimes physicians in this situation appear to be considering the job as a default option while backing out of a prior career mistake. To me that type of attitude suggests the risk of a second mistake, for the applicant and the company. There is no reason to paint a completely rosy picture over a negative experience; however, the focus should be on the future rather than the past.

While on interviews, I usually said that being a physician was not what I had originally anticipated. This generally was received with a series of understanding nods. I then sincerely said that I was looking for a job that could combine my medical expertise with my writing and creative interests. It is important to be honest, first with yourself, and then with the potential employer, when describing why you want to make a transition and why you are considering the current position. Too often people come in and say that they are "looking for new challenges," which is vague and clichéd.

I am generally looking for someone who has energy and passion. This comes across in different ways, and hopefully not through hyperbole or high-fiving during the interview. I usually look for this characteristic during a discussion about a side interest or hobby; ideally it also comes across about the position being discussed. Someone who does not demonstrate passion about a topic of interest will probably not be enthusiastic about their work.

It is extremely important to hire people that are team players.

Most applicants know this and come in saying repeatedly that they are a team player. This can sometimes have a negative effect when it comes across as being scripted. An experienced interviewer can sense fairly well whether someone will be a good team player, and usually this does not require the words "team player" being stated at any point. This is a particularly important point for physicians. Rather than sugar coating this, I think it is important to state honestly that this is a characteristic often lacking in physicians. Even some of the more easy going physicians have well established egos from being in the spotlight among their families and peers throughout their lives. This increases during clinical practice, where the physician is generally the focus of attention and the key decision maker.

The transition to a new job really requires checking your ego at the door. Someone who cannot work well in a team environment will generally not be successful in a company. This potential problem is often obvious during a telephone discussion or interview. Occasionally a physician will slip through the cracks and get into a working environment where their inflated ego and lack of team mentality will become problematic for an account, a group of employees, or even an entire company.

TRANSITION

How did you know that you were making the right decision?

It is nearly impossible to adequately convey what it was like to step across the threshold into a non-clinical job. I spent 18 years striving for a career in medicine and then practicing as a surgeon. During the last two years in practice, I diverted my focus toward something quite different. There were numerous decision points during those two years that got me progressively closer toward the new position. First, I decided that I wanted to leave clinical practice. It then took a fair amount of time before confirming that a career transition was feasible. Over time I honed in on a few particular types of positions, primarily within the medical communications industry. A Medical Director position within medical communications emerged as the most appropriate and desirable option.

Every decision point along the way was challenging but liberating. During this process I continuously re-evaluated my priority list. The realization that no job is perfect was somewhat disappointing but essential; I acknowledged that I would have to make sacrifices to achieve my goals. Withstanding a marked initial salary cut and commuting a long distance were sacrifices that I was willing to make for this particular position.

Despite this entire progression and ample preparation, accepting the job offer was one of the most frightening and exhilarating experiences of my life. There it was – the opportunity that I was waiting for. It

136

was becoming a reality. I knew I was making the right decision, but for the first time in my life I was unsure of the outcome. What would the new job really be like? What would the company be like? Did I calculate our financial situation accurately? How would this impact my family? What would my colleagues say? What would my patients say? These questions crept up 1,000 times during the previous two years, but now they were playing continuously in my head. The answers to some of these questions would come quickly enough; the answers to others would decrease in importance.

Confidence in my decision came through visualizing the worst case scenario and understanding that I would still have good options to recover. If I completely hated my new job, I could always pick up where I left off and join another practice or start my own. I made sure not to burn any bridges in this regard. I maintained my medical license and board status and held on to hospital affiliations for the longest time possible.

Do you remember when you decided to become a physician? It was probably something that you felt inside, not a calculation on a spreadsheet. There were probably inklings of uncertainty along the way, but deep down you knew you were making the right decision – the only decision. This is how I felt when entering medical communications. There were many unanswered questions, but I was doing the right thing.

I left medicine with the same degree of certainty that I once strove toward it. When I talk to people considering a career transition, I emphasize the fact that feeling scared is normal in a new setting, but that feeling as though you are settling for something is a warning signal. If you do your research along the way, accept that this will be a fairly time consuming process and avoid jumping at the first opportunity that arises, you will have a much better chance of succeeding and being happy in your new job.

QUESTION

How did your family react?

ANSWER

I published an article about the unique mixture of emotions that my family and I experienced during the career transition (It's Not Easy to Quit Medicine, *Medical Economics.* 2003;2:77).

My wife was as happy as I was about the career transition. Although she is not a physician, she survived four years of medical school, six years of training, and four years of clinical practice. She can read most x-rays, knows when and how to insert a chest tube, and still fields medical calls by friends and family. She felt the impact of clinical practice, for better and for worse, every step of the way.

My wife was more nervous for me than I was for myself, though. Maybe she has more sense than I do. She probably realized the extent of the risk I was taking at the time; only later did I look back and allow myself to think about it. Meanwhile, friends, family, and colleagues were asking her whether I was okay and voiced concern about my future earning potential in the new position. Luckily, any lingering doubts were wiped away during the first few months.

My parents were also always aware of my frustrations with clinical practice and my desire for a career transition. They were relieved when I made the transition, although they could still not explain to you what I do now.

An important factor in the decision to leave clinical practice was a desire to improve quality time with my family. I now enjoy infinitely better control over my schedule and no longer miss the important milestones and events in my kids' lives. Nevertheless, there have been several eye-opening moments along the way. When I first started as an Associate Medical Director, my middle daughter (then three years old) was upset that I would be working farther away and could not eat lunch with her at the office. I was expecting a different reaction from my oldest daughter (then 7 years old). She was old enough to understand how much my surgery career imposed upon our lives. "In my new job," I assured her, "no one will page me when we're together and make me come back in to work. We can make weekend plans, go out to dinner. That's great, isn't it?" She looked up at me with disappointment and said, "You mean you're not going to be taking care of patients anymore?"

My youngest daughter (now 5 years old) was born after I left my practice. As a result, I see her much more than I saw the older two when they were her age. She asked me to come into her pre-K class to tell them about my job. Of course I was delighted, but then she said, "Don't tell them about your job now. Tell them what you used to do . . . when you were a doctor . . . and you helped kids." I never imagined that my kids paid much attention to my career, but they were obviously proud of what I did.

Many of my relatives were surprised and disappointed by my career transition. I used to have the longest name in my family – "Mike he's the doctor the one I was telling you about". Grandparents and parents are particularly proud of a child who grows up to be a physician. I think that no matter what happens to the healthcare system or to the profession of medicine itself, that fact will never change. The importance of the profession is undeniable; leaving clinical practice sacrifices some of this prestige.

QUESTION

How did your colleagues react?

ANSWER

The first physician that I told of my career transition was the chief partner in my practice. As I was telling him I was leaving his group, I could see his obvious disappointment from a business standpoint. When I told him that I was leaving clinical practice altogether, he was profoundly disappointed. He was completely incredulous and spent the next several days speaking with me, not about staying with the practice, but about remaining a surgeon.

The physicians and other staff in my practice were equally shocked by my decision. People could not believe that I would leave my clinical practice and had difficulty understanding what I was going to be doing in my new job. Many of them remain convinced that I became a pharmaceutical sales representative, and others think that I am a novelist.

One of my former mentors actually got angry with my decision and accused me of wasting the time he spent training me. This physician has always regretted not spending enough time with his children – a vision of how my life might have been if I continued along my clinical practice path. I had to ignore his comment and move forward. I actually felt sorry for him.

When I am speaking with physicians about my new industry, there is an interesting transition that typically occurs mid-conversation. In the beginning when I mention that I used to be a plastic surgeon, they stare at me, baffled as to why I would want to leave that specialty. I can see them flipping through the files in their head, trying to sort through the possible reasons why I would have done this. They must assume that such a decision could not be voluntary. Then I describe the details of what I do in my job. At some point the confusion, or pessimism, or sarcasm, converts over and they ask whether there are additional positions open. They will probably not end up transitioning careers, but they seem to have a better understanding of why I did. (They probably then go out and tell their colleagues that they met this guy who used to be a plastic surgeon and now is a pharmaceutical sales representative or something like that.)

Then of course, there are the physicians who have been speaking about leaving their practices for years. A couple of friends in this situation looked on and cheered as I made the big transition. In fact, one plastic surgeon even sends me articles about cosmetic surgery complications and lawsuits, telling me to hold onto them in case I ever lose my mind and consider going back into practice.

QUESTION

Did you have to take a pay cut?

ANSWER

Financial considerations were not a primary driving factor as I left clinical practice, although I needed to meet certain short term and long term thresholds. Based on my family's historical and projected spending, I calculated the lowest salary level that I could tolerate during the first year. The initial goal was to get a job with a salary that could sustain our lifestyle without resulting in a net loss. The target salary that we calculated ended up being fairly accurate.

Despite all of our best laid plans, however, my initial position in medical communications paid less than our magic number. This presented a real challenge from a financial standpoint and a difficult decision for me. I was able to negotiate a timeline for performance-based salary increases over the first year. These scheduled increases would still leave me $10,000 below my threshold for breaking even one year into my new job. My wife and I carefully assessed this together. Despite a projected net loss during the first two years and a certain level of future risk, we agreed that accepting this position was still the right decision.

I gave up one-third of my salary between my last year in clinical practice and my first year in medical communications. We were below the threshold for breaking even and, as expected, began to eat into our savings. This time was reminiscent of my last two years in residency, during which we had to take out loans in order to make ends meet.   The financial situation was even more frightening in this case, however, because I was not sure what my earning potential would be shortly after that initial period. What if my salary peaked at little more than the initial agreement?

The financial aspects of my decision at the time would probably make an accountant cry. While considering non-clinical options, I was a plastic surgeon doing mostly hand surgery. If I continued my current practice, my earning potential would have been pretty generous and within a fairly predictable range. I did weigh the option of making changes in my practice. If I switched to a primarily cosmetic surgery patient mix, my earning potential would have skyrocketed over the next several years. As I entered medical communications I was fairly certain that my earning potential would never reach that of a hand surgeon. It seemed like a guarantee that I would not come anywhere close to what I would have earned as a cosmetic surgeon. Despite my assessment of the financial situation, I chose to make a career transition because of all the other factors affecting my decision.

QUESTION

How did you feel during the transition?

ANSWER

Leaving clinical practice was like finally breaking the surface and emerging into the sunlight after holding my breath under water for years.

I felt stuck for so long, as though I had spent most of my life moving in the wrong direction. I was frustrated with myself. How could I become so trapped? I was intelligent, driven, and hard-working. There were few outlets to discuss my frustration. During the search, I had to keep my plans from colleagues and patients, for fear of prematurely losing my practice referral base. Besides, being a physician is something toward which many people aspire; we are thought to exist on a higher plane, one immune to the emotional stress. Physicians who express frustration with their job are considered to be whining.

Another physician who is considering leaving practice recently told me that he hid his feelings even from his wife because he was embarrassed by no longer wanting to a practice medicine. He referred to the day that he first broached the topic with her as his "coming out of the closet."

My career transition was liberating. For the first time since starting medical school, I was extremely excited about my future career path. Interestingly, medical communications would draw upon my knowledge from the past. Leaving clinical practice would not mean that my past efforts in medicine would be thrown away. I was not going to be "wasting all those years of training." The impact of this awareness is difficult to put into words. Perhaps more than anything, though, I was able to "come out of the closet" with regard to my desire to leave clinical practice. By speaking openly about my career, I could be myself again.

QUESTION

How did you know you were choosing the right job?

ANSWER

I applied for several positions during my two year job search. Many of these were not in the medical communications industry. As I filled out various applications, I struggled to explain why I was interested in these particular jobs. In retrospect, I think that most of those jobs would have provided me with a place to run from my clinical practice, rather than the promise of exciting new opportunities.

The job in medical communications offered me an opportunity to achieve all of the objectives on my priority list. I would be able to combine my past medical expertise and love for writing in order to move in this new direction. Most importantly, when I pictured myself in this new career, I was excited. For the first time, I was sure that I was headed toward something rewarding, instead of only leaving an unwanted situation. I had not felt that way since I walked into an operating room for the first time.

While recognizing that my next job might not be my final career destination, I was satisfied with the knowledge that I was moving in the right direction. Once again, I took out the list of my optimal job characteristics and scored the new job against my clinical practice. The new job score was not perfect, but the improvement was convincing.

Figure 8. Assessing the Job Opportunity

My List

Optimal Job Characteristics	Clinical Practice	Non-Clinical Job #1
Intellectual Challenge	4/5	3/5
Team Environment	2/5	4/5
Sense of Accomplishment	4/5	3/5
Financial Reward	3/5	2/5
Manageable Workload	2/5	4/5
Schedule Control	1/5	4/5
TOTAL	16/30	20/30

Your List

Optimal Job Characteristics	Clinical Practice	Non-Clinical Job #1
	/5	/5
	/5	/5
	/5	/5
	/5	/5
	/5	/5
	/5	/5
TOTAL	/30	/30

QUESTION

Where you nervous?

ANSWER

You bet I was.

QUESTION

Should I maintain my board certification and medical license?

ANSWER

There are several reasons to maintain your board certification status. The first is that, as horrible as this may be sound, it is feasible that you may decide to return to your clinical practice after a trial period in a new job. Even if you want to do a smaller amount of part-time work, such as a half day per week or a day per month in a clinic, maintaining your board status will be important. Also, there are a growing number of non-profit organizations providing medical services. If you would like to spend a week or two annually or even more time with one of these groups, board certification may be required.

I maintained my plastic and hand surgery board certification, which has proven to be very helpful. During the few years following my career transition, I went to South America on hand surgery missions with Interplast, a non-profit organization providing operations and education around the world. Interplast requires board certification in plastic surgery or a related specialty. Being involved with this organization allowed me to continue using my surgical skills and provide medical services to people, much in the way that I thought I would be doing when I chose surgery as a profession many years earlier.

It may be helpful to inquire with your specialty board as to whether there is an alternative status for non-clinical physicians, since this may allow you to maintain your certification at reduced cost. You should also be aware of the CME and re-certification requirements of your specialty. It is easy to lose track of such details once you become focused on the new job.

You should also check into the benefits provided by your new company, since some employers provide reimbursement for education and professional costs, including CME requirements, medical licenses, and board fees. Remaining up to date on such items may be beneficial in your new job. For example, if you are a cardiologist working in the cardiovascular therapeutic area within the pharmaceutical industry, your company may prefer that you maintain your board certification. Some of the benefit may be intangible, such as increased credibility when interacting with physician peers.

Similar questions have come up regarding maintaining a medical license. Many of the reasons for maintaining board certification also apply to maintaining a medical license. This also keeps your options open as far as potential part-time activities as well as prescription writing ability. Most states also have an option of placing a medical license on inactive status, allowing activation much faster and easier than reapplying later on.

Whether to maintain your medical malpractice insurance depends on the nature of your current coverage and the likelihood that you will be practicing part-time or writing prescriptions for any reason. If neither of these is the case, then medical malpractice insurance is generally not necessary. Congratulations – one of the most detested aspects of modern medical practice may soon be   behind you.

A key consideration with regard to these decisions is the difficulty in obtaining a medical license and board certification in the first place. I am sure that, like me, you would rather err on the side of paying some extra money for a while, rather than going through the application/certification process again. For this reason, it is probably best to maintain license and board status until you become firmly grounded in your new job.

Similarly, you should probably maintain your hospital privileges as long as possible. Again, the potential trouble of reapplying outweighs whatever additional paperwork and cost are associated with maintaining staff privileges. I was able to convert to courtesy staff status for about a year, but then policy changes requiring malpractice coverage forced me to resign. By that point, however, I was established in my new job and comfortable with the decision to sever this tie to clinical practice.

Keep in mind that your first non-clinical job should not be the exclusive driver for your decisions regarding licensure and certification. A common initial misperception is that leaving clinical practice leads directly to the ultimate job – the culmination of the quest. After making the clinical to non-clinical transition, which feels like a quantum leap at the time, physicians often see their careers in a different way and have their eyes open for further opportunities. They understand that the first non-clinical job is probably not their last, and they are at least comfortable, perhaps even excited, by that possibility. Holding onto those painstakingly obtained licenses, certifications, and hospital privileges may help in ways that are not apparent today.

QUESTION

What were the first few weeks like in your new job?

ANSWER

I was immediately happy with my decision. Everything was new and exciting. My co-workers were great. There was a lot to learn in the new position, on my particular accounts, and about the industry as a whole. The client on my first account valued my input. The period immediately following a career transition produces an unfamiliar combination of vulnerability and insecurity, and getting positive feedback from co-workers and clients helps smooth the way.

Being confident to ask questions when I did not understand something helped a great deal. There is a large amount of lingo indigenous to each industry, representing the equivalent of a foreign language to an outsider. I remember being in meetings during the first few weeks, hearing streams of abbreviations and acronyms and often feeling lost in the conversation. It took a while before I was speaking the same language as everyone else.

I had a couple of mentors within the company as I was getting started, and they helped me a great deal. I took every opportunity to learn from them and worked as hard as I could to convince them that they had made a smart hire. Making my managers look good ensured that my efforts would be recognized and well received.

QUESTION

In what ways do physicians struggle after transitioning?

ANSWER

Most physicians will deny having a big ego, perhaps because there is always another physician next to them that has an even bigger ego. (Of course, I am the exception).

Physicians' egos may cause problems that are easily perceptible to their team but not self-apparent. Although a rare individual may make ridiculous demands and boss around their co-workers, the vast majority of issues that arise are more subtle. Physicians who show up late for meetings, miss deadlines, or decline requests for support made by a superior or another team member demonstrate an underlying feeling that their co-workers' time is less important than theirs.

In any industry there are issues that arise that are considered to be "emergencies." When such an "emergency" is brought to my attention, I often remind the person that a true emergency is when someone is rushed in by ambulance with an ax sticking out of their head. Of course I then reassure them that I understand the level of urgency of the matter and will take care of the problem accordingly. Non-clinical physicians get into trouble when they fail to treat such an issue with an appropriate level of urgency. Everyone is offended when a physician is condescending or acts as though their current industry is not as important as their previous work. Physicians who are the most successful in their new industries are those who roll up their sleeves and pitch in to help out their team, even when the immediate task at hand seems below their "job description."

Transitioning from a clinical practice where the physician is always right to a business where the customer is always right can present problems. There are times in medical communications, for example, when a Medical Director is certain that the client is making an incorrect decision. Voicing a differing opinion in such cases is expected; however, in the end the client has to be allowed to make the final decision in most cases. Knowing when to express your opinion and when to remain quiet is important.

THE OTHER SIDE

QUESTION

What is your industry – medical communications?

ANSWER

It really was not until making a career transition to medical communications that I realized the extent of the industry and the many sub-components that exist. Some companies work across several of these categories, but others are highly specialized within one or two specific areas. These specific components include medical advertising, promotional and CME medical education content, publication planning, general meeting logistics, public relations, and other types of specialty medical programs. There are even some companies that become sub-specialized, focusing on particular therapeutic areas, healthcare groups such as nurses, or non-profit organizations. Others provide specific expertise in areas such as managed care. New niche areas are arising on a regular basis, expanding the numerous opportunities already available.

My first non-clinical job was in a medical advertising agency. We developed strategic marketing plans, including product positioning statements, brand personality maps, written briefs, and ad concepts to be used by pharmaceutical product teams as a guide for developing tactics. We then created advertisements placed in medical journals, as well as many types of educational materials and brochures delivered by pharmaceutical sales representatives to physicians and other healthcare personnel. We worked with graphic artists to develop images and videos to depict the mechanism of action of medications, some of my favorite projects. We also developed slides for CME symposia and promotional events such as dinner meetings and teleconferences. As an Associate Medical Director, I worked with a medical team of writers, editors, a creative team of copy writers and artists, and an account team that handled the business aspects and project management of our work. I was responsible for the quality and accuracy of all medical content on my accounts.

My second job was at a large company that focused primarily on medical education. There was a logistics component to the company, with many employees dedicated to coordinating physician travel arrangements to attend educational meetings. The division initially worked on both promotional and CME content, until delegating these components to separate divisions to meet industry guidelines. We then focused on content for promotional meetings (eg, slides, monographs, advisory board executive summaries, and other handout materials).

Our division also provided publication planning services. This work involves assessing available and future clinical trial data, mapping out a plan for where to present and publish such data, and then providing writing and editorial support to a variety of projects, such as abstracts, posters, oral presentations, and manuscripts.

My company, Peloton Advantage, is scientifically driven and provides publication planning and medical content development services to pharmaceutical and biotechnology companies. We primarily hire physicians for Medical Director positions, similar to my   previous jobs.

QUESTION

Are your hours better?

ANSWER

Most people who ask me this question generally mean "Are you working fewer hours?" In general it was never really the total number of hours that was a problem when I was in practice. I was probably working 50 to 60 hours most weeks, which seemed like a reasonable time commitment, considering my financial compensation. What I really did not like was the unpredictability of my hours. Frequent calls forced me back to my office or the emergency room, even when I was not on call. Interrupted meals and limited sleep were the rule, rather than the exception. I never knew when one of those calls would change my day. I rarely left town or even made local plans on the weekend; my beeper was a ball and chain.

Immediately after entering medical communications, my working hours were markedly reduced and much more predictable. I was working a "9 to 5" job for the first time in my life, with few urgent matters arising and very little travel. I know physicians in non-clinical jobs who continue to work such hours, so this type of lifestyle is definitely possible on a sustained basis. In general, though, "9 to 5" contributors tend to stay in the same positions, without much salary increase over time. After the career transition, my financial situation required increasing my salary within the first few years in order to exceed our cost of living threshold again. As a result, I progressively worked harder and took on more responsibilities, such as involvement in new business development for the company. Of course, this increased my overall number of hours.

Even when working longer hours, I completely owned my off time. As a result, I was finally able to fulfill basic family responsibilities and confidently plan activities and trips. My life felt normal for the first time since leaving medical school. The difference between working long but predictable hours vs long unpredictable hours was dramatic for me. Despite my willingness to work hard, I was very happy that clinical practice was no longer invading my private time.

Later, in a management position at a second company, my total number of hours increased exponentially and I was often taking work home in order to keep up. Urgent requests from senior management came in an unpredictable pattern and infringed upon my private life and plans. I was also traveling much more than ever before. Luckily, several levels of promotion and markedly increased financial compensation accompanied these drawbacks. This management experience also paved the way toward the next step of my career, which was to start my own business. The expression "no pain, no gain" applies to most aspects of life, and certainly to the business world.

Now, as a business owner, I work about as many hours as I did in practice. Regardless of the total number of hours, however, I have more control over my work week than ever before. I attend events at my children's school. Weekend plans are never interrupted by emergency telephone calls. My free time is my own; the job does not interfere with my family life.

QUESTION

Are you now making as much money as you would have in practice?

ANSWER

I have had a lot of surprises in my new industry, some good and some bad. By far the biggest surprise, and the most pleasant, has been regarding the compensation that physicians can achieve outside of clinical practice. When I left my practice, I was convinced that I was giving up a large earning potential. Following the expected drop in salary, however, my compensation during the subsequent years has exceeded my projected earning potential as a practicing clinician. Although I acknowledge that my trajectory has exceeded that of the average physician in medical communications, I have learned that non-clinical jobs generally pay much more money than I ever would have anticipated.

While it is difficult to predict the success of a company, which could thrive or fail over any period of time, owning a business has erased any cap on my future earning potential. I now have confidence that my future earnings can far exceed any amount I could have achieved in clinical practice.

QUESTION

Do you have any regrets?

ANSWER

Definitely not.

Leaving clinical practice to enter medical communications was one of the best decisions of my life. Going into medicine was a great choice as well. The outcome (so far) is simply not what I pictured when I went into medical school.

There was a long period of time during my residency and clinical practice when I was feeling lost, confused and frustrated. Even during that time, however, I felt as though my job was more interesting and rewarding than what everyone around me was doing. I still knew that there was a much better job for me somewhere but basically had no idea what it was.

As I entered my new job I realized that all of the different pieces of my life were coming together. I could shift my focus from the past to the present and future. If I could look back, snap my fingers, and somehow have an MD/MBA degree from Columbia instead of just my MD, perhaps that would be nice. Removing a few years of my training or a couple of years in practice might have been beneficial. But what would have been different in a negative way if I had done such things? Maybe if I left practice two years earlier I would not have been as certain about my career transition. Maybe I would have missed out on additional management skills that later affected my ability to take on a leadership position in my new industry.

Getting stuck too much in the past can interfere with decisions today. I learn a lot from talking with physicians considering a career transition. Many are hesitating because of a subconscious sense that making such a change would redefine a portion of their past experience as irrelevant, unnecessary, or simply a mistake. Physicians are extremely averse to making mistakes. To me the only mistake would have been missing the opportunity in front of me. The best way to achieve goals and gain satisfaction is to identify and explore the open paths today, rather than worry about how you got to that fork in the path.

QUESTION

What do you like best about your job?

ANSWER

I like almost everything about medical communications. Fortunately I discovered in this industry a career path that combined two of my passions – medicine and writing. My career transition became an essential step in a natural evolution, rather than a desperate attempt to back out of a dead end. I no longer saw myself as "changing careers." I was taking multiple sets of experiences and interests and merging them together in a unique way to open a career path that I never would have imagined. The spark was finally back in the relationship with my career. I enjoyed going to work again.

My job is intellectually challenging. I now work across nearly every disease state, which requires a great deal of reading and learning in therapeutic areas far outside of my recent surgical expertise. My scientific and clinical understanding of various diseases is now much greater than when I was in practice. Not since internship have I absorbed so much new information.

Work in medical communications is quite varied, due to the number of therapeutic areas and types of projects that are involved. On a given day, I may be doing scientific writing, meeting with clients, or participating in an advisory board discussion with the top thought leader physicians in a particular area. On some days I do a little bit of each.

I recently went back to my optimal job characteristics list and scored my second job in medical communications and my current role as a business owner. The progression has been interesting. The improved score as I left clinical practice was impressive. The management role in my second medical communications job brought more responsibility and a needed improvement in financial compensation, along with a much higher workload and reduced control over my schedule when compared to my first non-clinical job. The improvement in my scoring system was only slight, but the experience prepared to start a business. My current scores far exceed those of my clinical practice experience.

Figure 9. Side By Side Job Comparison

Optimal Job Characteristics	Clinical Practice	Non-Clinical Job #1	Non-Clinical Job #2	Business Owner
Intellectual Challenge	4/5	3/5	4/5	4/5
Team Environment	2/5	4/5	3/5	4/5
Sense of Accomplishment	4/5	3/5	4/5	5/5
Financial Reward	3/5	2/5	4/5	4/5
Manageable Workload	2/5	4/5	3/5	4/5
Schedule Control	1/5	4/5	3/5	4/5
TOTAL	16/30	20/30	21/30	25/30

QUESTION

Is there anything that you do not like about your job?

ANSWER

There is no such thing as a perfect job, but you can get pretty close. I love medical communications and the company that I own; however, there are still aspects of the job that I dislike. My commute ranges anywhere from one to two hours each way, every day. Obviously, I could very easily move with my family and live close to my job. This would eliminate the entire commuting problem but would create other issues, so it is something we have not done yet.

Working particularly hard for a patient who did not seem to recognize or appreciate my efforts always frustrated me. The bad news is that once you go to a different type of job, it is just as likely that your hard work will not always be recognized by managers, co-workers or clients. One of the things that I have learned from being in different industries and companies is that some of the aspects that we tend to dislike about our jobs are simply a part of human nature and therefore ubiquitous. Try not to blame such problems on the job itself.

Remember – if a truly perfect job existed, it would probably get a little boring after a while, thus making it imperfect.

QUESTION

What is different about a non-clinical job?

ANSWER

The most important difference is the degree of control that I have over my personal life. Most physicians are willing to work hard, but not having control of our personal lives is distressing. I am now very satisfied to be doing work that is challenging and interesting but does not prevent me from enjoying time with my family.

Another major difference involves the team dynamic. When I was in clinical practice I was the authority in most situations. The office staff did what I asked of them. The operating room staff did what I asked of them. I wrote "orders" in hospital charts, and they were followed. Patients even occasionally followed my recommendations.

In a team environment in an office setting, a physician's opinion is only one of several in the room. There have been many times when the plan of action differed from my recommendation. Sometimes I was right; sometimes I was wrong. Even when I disagreed with the plan, however, it was important to contribute my best effort to obtain the team's goal. Some physicians in clinical practice who are considering a career transition minimize the effect that this group dynamic will have on them, but I often wonder whether their egos can actually tolerate the blow. In the end, of course, the client or customer will have the final say.

Job security is another difference. When was the last time you worried about job security? When I was in clinical practice, job security was a complete non-issue. How could I lose my job? The demand for my expertise was constantly increasing in clinical practice, which was part of the challenge of maintaining an even balance of career and personal life. Although my position has never been terminated, I have seen the impact of this for others on several occasions. Each of the companies where I was an employee had several rounds of layoffs.

The issue of job security remains as one climbs the corporate ladder. While the most valuable people are generally spared from layoffs, sometimes the accountants target the highest salaries in an attempt to reduce expenses. By far the worst part of being in a management position at the previous company where I worked was the need to lay off co-workers. I had to lay off several members of the medical staff – even people that I hired and a few physicians. Although these are business decisions, the impact is obviously quite personal.

QUESTION

Do you feel like you wasted all that training?

ANSWER

There it is. Nearly every person I have talked to about my career transition has either asked this question or considered asking it. When people ask that question, they view the career transition as evidence of an earlier mistake, and therefore my clinical experience as wasted. Back when I was feeling lost in my practice and searching for a new job I might have felt differently, but today the answer is an emphatic "no."

I continue to use my medical knowledge every day. With the exception of cutting people open, excising or repairing tissues, and sewing them back together again, I use all of the major skills that I learned throughout my training and my experience as a clinician. I know that I would not be as successful in my current position or as an entrepreneur without that experience. Internship alone coated me with a layer of Teflon that protects me from any challenge, stress, or abuse that any other job could throw at me. What could compare to that?

Even if I had transitioned to a career path that was completely unrelated to my medical background, I would not consider the earlier years wasted. Practicing medicine is a truly unique experience, complete with the highest emotional pinnacles that a person can achieve, as well as some of the greatest emotional challenges possible. The goals I set for myself as a teenager provided an interesting first phase in my career, a decade of clinical experience, and a sense of accomplishment. A career is one facet of the non-linear journey through life, and trying too hard to force-fit it all into a master plan will interfere with the experience. The residual calculating surgeon in me might be embarrassed to share such a philosophical assessment, but I am a little older and wiser than I was when I was in practice.

I have actually continued use my surgical skills in a unique way through my involvement with Interplast. A non-profit surgical organization that travels to foreign countries, Interplast provides various types of reconstructive plastic surgery operations and professional education. I have gone to La Paz, Bolivia twice on hand surgery trips. Being involved with this organization allowed me to continue using my surgical skills and provide medical care to people, much in the way that I always thought I would be doing – without the cumbersome inundation of paperwork or insurance company restrictions.

If you are considering leaving clinical practice and still feel as though you have wasted your training, give it some time. Your perspective will change in a few years. If that is not comforting enough to hear, just think of the endless supply of tasteless cocktail party stories you will have to tell for many years ahead. You would not have those without your clinical experience.

QUESTION

What have been the biggest surprises since your career transition?

ANSWER

I have had a few big surprises. The first one was how many different types of non-clinical opportunities are available to a physician and how many people are actually out there doing these jobs. Working in my practice provided no exposure to these types of industries. Making the transition into medical communications was like traveling into a different dimension where endless opportunity exists for physicians.

Another big surprise was seeing what I could personally accomplish outside the area that had been my single line of focus for many years. Change, in itself, is one of the biggest challenges that we face. My career transition was a challenging, and in some ways frightening, experience. Eight years ago I did not know that my current industry even existed. Now I own a medical communications company.

A very pleasant surprise was the financial compensation achievable in a non-clinical job. Non-clinical salaries are much higher than I ever thought possible. While financial considerations were never a driving force for me, the limitations that I anticipated were an initial barrier for me making the career transition. In retrospect I am very happy that I took the calculated risk despite this perceived obstacle.

QUESTION

Looking back on the transition, what would you do differently now?

ANSWER

Much of my job search was inefficient.

Figuring out where to focus my efforts was a challenge. As a result, I spent countless evenings inefficiently surfing the Internet, and even applied for jobs not appropriately suited to my expertise and interests. The only information helpful to a physician considering a career transition was scattered across disparate web sites. It took two years of digging and ongoing time afterwards to gather these fragments.

Today I would be much more aggressive at networking. During my job search, I had to overcome my introversion. Being timid and feeling as though I was imposing on people slowed me down. It took a while to realize that others were actually happy to help me. The system that I used was effective, but there were many times when I put new names on my call list for the following week, rather than picking up the phone right away and establishing the next contacts. I think if I had been more aggressive and confident in calling those people, the networking process would have expanded exponentially in a short amount of time, rather than at the rate that it did. In fact, I could have accomplished even more of the search process through networking.

In response to these voids in information and networking access, I created Physician Renaissance Network (www.prnresource.com), a comprehensive resource for physicians with non-clinical careers or interests. Hopefully the information on the web site will provide other physicians with a resource that I needed but never found.

QUESTION

What advice do you have for physicians considering a career transition?

ANSWER

The most important advice that I can provide is to do a systematic review of potential options. Once people decide that they are inadequately satisfied with their career, they often become impatient to make a change. The search process needs to follow a series of steps. The first assessment is to weigh the various priorities in your life and decide whether any career transition is a reasonable option. From that point it is important to identify what the realistic options are. Identify the general industry and type of work first; only then it is time to assess which specific companies and positions to target.

Hold off on job inquiry letters, resumes, and applications until you are sure about what you want to do. A well-informed applicant makes the best applicant. Someone who simply knows that they want to leave but is not really sure where they are headed is not very convincing in an interview. More importantly, a premature application and interview may actually lead to a job offer that could force a premature and potentially poor decision.

The career transition should feel as right as your original choice to go into medicine. If the search process ends up reassuring you that clinical practice is still the best option, or maybe that you can even improve your current situation, then that in itself is a valuable realization. On the other hand, if the search does identify a position that can provide an opportunity to begin focusing on the future, rather than feeling trapped in the present, then you will be one of the lucky ones. You will have found the sign post to your future career path.

Keep your eyes and options open, and enjoy the evolution of your career!

ABOUT THE AUTHOR

Michael J. McLaughlin, MD, is co-founder of Peloton Advantage (pelotonadvantage.com), a medical communications company. He received degrees from Harvard College and Columbia University. After four years as a plastic surgeon and hand specialist, he networked through a career change into medical communications. Along the way, he also founded Physician Renaissance Network (PRNresource.com), a free resource for doctors with non-clinical careers and interests, and wrote the book *Do You Feel Like You Wasted All That Training?* His novels include the medical thriller, *Extinction*, and the innovative and controversial story, *The Satin Strangler Blogs*. He lives in New Jersey with his wife and 3 daughters.